Change for Burma
Change for World

Oscar Aye Myint

Swan Tha Khin

Oscar Aye Myint

Oscar Aye Myint Publishing

PO Box 350420

Brooklyn, NY 11235-0420

oscarayemyint@gmail.com

ISBN: 069256683X
ISBN-13: 978-0692566831

For Burmese citizens, go to www.minthakhinusa.com. On September 8th, 2015, this website was formed and the *Campaign for Aung San Suu Kyi* speech was put on the site. The issues and subjects that were discussed in the speech are below:

❖ Myanmar's brief history

❖ What happened to Myanmar under the military rule

❖ In 1990, the NLD Party won the election, but the military government did not transfer power as promised, and the NLD party members were placed in jail

❖ In 2010, another election occurred in Myanmar while the NLD Party was still in jail. The military government conducted this election unlawfully because they are not in fact the true elected government for Myanmar.

❖ There is no law nor justice in Myanmar

❖ Open Letter to United Nations

❖ Why the military government's constitution in Myanmar is unlawful

❖ Farmers' properties in Myanmar are being forcefully taken away unlawfully

❖ The military government has guaranteed that the citizens will be wealthy. Independent rule in all states and a real federal system are also being promised.

❖ Why free education and free medical care must exist

❖ How to support Myanmar's economy without foreign investments

❖ Why you should support Aung San Suu Kyi

PEACE

All nations need peace. Without peace, a nation cannot develop and evolve. The reason for this is because no matter how rich you are, if there is a war, you can lose everything you have very quickly. You can become a refugee anytime. No matter how healthy you are, if there is a war you can be killed at any time. That is why for every human being on this planet, peace is the first priority.

In Myanmar right now, the general elections have begun in order for people to gain peace. But criminals have been released from jail often which is causing more crimes in Myanmar, and disrupting the peace. The only people who hold guns in Myanmar are the army and revolutionists. Who has responsibility for a civil war and peace in Myanmar?

DEMOCRACY

What is truth? A truth is something the majority will agree to accept. If the majority agrees to accept it, it must be the truth. That is the meaning of democracy to me.

I want there to be a democracy in Myanmar. That's why I want the NLD party who fights for democracy to win the elections.

STATE'S POWER

State's powers are not personal belongings. It's something the citizens choose to give through elections. It's only due to the citizen's votes and permission that one gains state power. Because the world regards this as the truth, most nations hold elections. That's why for dictatorships to continue holding power is impossible for the world's future.

CHANGE

Demand for change is not the fault of the people who demand it. The current situation calls for change and therefore there needs to be change. If the current situation benefits the citizens, no one will demand for change.

Myanmar's military rule has lasted for over 50 years. Under their control, the country has become broken. There is no democracy, no human rights, and no freedom. That's why people demand for change in Myanmar.

The military government is afraid to change because in the past, they've committed atrocities against the citizens. Their fear for retaliation from the Myanmar's citizens is unneeded and offensive to the Myanmar citizens' character because the citizens are not as barbaric as the government seems to think they are. Revenge continues to breed hate forever. It's the wrong thing. Punishment and justice serve to satisfy the victims. However it is not an equal payment for the victims because in Myanmar, there is no Hammurabi's Law. That's why they must negotiate with the citizens to create peace that satisfies the peoples' desires.

PUBLIC PROPERTY

Natural resources, taxes from citizens, and the country's budget are all the public property. The citizens own it. That's why when using public property, it must be at the citizens' agreement because the real owners are the citizens. For example, if my property were being used by somebody else without my permission, I won't be able to accept it. Just like this, when using the public property that belong to the citizens, it must be agreed to by the citizens. It's better that way.

In Myanmar, the citizens' land is being taken away under the guise of "projects" by the government without the citizens' agreement. This is very wrong and is also against the law. All of this land is not the government's property.

CITZENS AND GOVERNMENT

In a nation, there must be agreement between the citizens and the government. If not, there will be conflict. There won't be peace, the country won't develop, everything will be in turmoil. A government is there because of the citizens. If there are no citizens, there will be no government. That's why a government needs citizens. There are many many families and citizens in a nation. That's why there is a need for a government to rule them in order to keep structure and peace. Therefore why the government and citizens both need each other, and must exist at each other's agreement in order for there to be peace.

In Myanmar, the military government has controlled the nation for over 50 years. There is often conflict between the citizens and the government because the citizens did not agree to the dictatorship system they are ruled by.

JUSTICE

In every nation there is law and justice. Justice must be fair, true, precise, and without bias according to law. Bullying and killing their own citizens is unlawful. It is better to rule lawfully.

All humans must die. There is no need to kill when they are destined to die one day either way. That's why the government must rule according to the law.

In Myanmar, the military government has bullied, tortured, and killed their own citizens. Justice and fair rule has been lost in Myanmar for so long.

ORDER AND DUTY

Orders must be followed, and duties must be done. This is the mentality in all armies. A soldier has a brain, but cannot decide. A soldier has a heart, but cannot feel. The brain and the heart are taken out for soldiers to follow orders like a robot. That's why dictatorships use these innocent, brave, and noble soldiers to continuously rule a nation. I don't want to blame soldiers for following orders because they are noble people.

In Myanmar under a misguided rule, the soldiers are following misguided orders, and undertake the wrong duties. This creates suffering for the innocent citizens.

WHO IS IMPORTANT

All human beings living on this planet are important. They are created equal. For there to be food there needs to be farmers and fishermen. To educate the new generation, there needs to be teachers. To cure and care for ill, there needs to be doctors and nurses. Engineers, artists, lawyers, inventors, creators, workers, etc. are all needed in order for the nation to function and thrive. We need soldiers to protect the nation. And so everyone in their own way is valuable and important.

However in Myanmar, everyone is nothing with the exception of soldiers. The soldiers have more advantages and opportunities than everyone else. They've brainwashed the citizens by stating they are important and necessary for the nation's protection, that they are the most important. They want to lead and rule the country one after the other. They don't want to give their positions to other people. I respect and honor them for protecting the country, and sacrificing for the nation. But they are not free. The country pays their salary for them to live. That's why they're doing their jobs; it is their duty to protect the country because out of so many other occupations it is by their own free will that they chose to be soldiers. There is no mandatory military service in Myanmar.

POLITICIANS & REVOLUTIONARIES

Politician has no need to sacrifice. To win elections, they have to campaign. Their supporters donate money to them, and they use that to fund their campaigns. Once they win, they will also get a salary from the nation. At the end of their career, they get pensions. That's why politicians do not lose. I don't want to blame them. This is what is occurring all over the world, it's just the way things are.

But it is different for revolutionaries. They have to fight against the system which the citizens are dissatisfied with. They face many dangerous situations, and have sacrificed for their cause.

Aung San Suu Kyi is not a politician; she is a revolutionary. That's why she's the true leader for Myanmar.

THE WORLD IS EVOLVING

Some people in this world create resources for others to use. They make medicines, foods, technology, etc., for human beings. However others' creations are to hurt and kill human beings. One bullet can kill one person. They want many people to be killed so they create more bullets, chemical weapons, nuclear, etc. I think there's enough weapons now to kill all 6 billion human beings living on this planet.

That's why I think people create so many materials to use these days, but their mentality and sympathy has decreased. When there is a conflict put on the table, it's possible to peacefully negotiate and discuss to find a solution. However, they kill each other, and many many innocent people are suffering and dying. Has the world really evolved then?

In Myanmar, the military government and the revolutionaries even after 50 years are still fighting. Countless lives have been lost. In the same nation, brother against brother, they are killing each other. This is the result of a dictatorship system. This is the dictatorship system's "solution." All this must end in order to create a peaceful nation.

Oscar Aye Myint

Preface

Once upon a time, Myanmar had been ruled by a monarchy. For many centuries, this system persisted. Myanmar had been a prosperous nation under this system, it was in its Golden Age. But Myanmar became a colony of the British, and later was ruled under a fascist system by the Japanese. The different ethnic provinces of Myanmar banded together then and gained independence. After they gained independence, another government system was created to govern Myanmar. The government used a parliament democracy to rule the nation. While the new government was governing, the military planned a coup d'état and forcefully took over the nation. The military government has been ruling Myanmar since then under a dictatorship. Under their control, the country was in turmoil. There was always violence between the citizens and the military. There was often problems with the university students especially, and many were killed by the military during protests, creating a bloodbath.

In 1988, one of the most prominent uprisings in history occurred in Myanmar. It had been led by university students. The protests coincided with Aung San Suu Kyi's personal visit to Myanmar, and she became a leader for the citizens who were against the dictatorship system. She's still fighting for the nation's freedom from the military government today.

Under the dictatorship system in Myanmar, I experienced life as a student, farmer, government worker, and lawyer. This is my story.

I want everyone to have peace in the world because I am a human being too. Especially in Myanmar because I am Burmese.

Oscar Aye Myint

CONTENTS

CHAPTER 1
THE EXPLOSION AT SUNDOWN

"A gun does not shoot to the skies, it shoots straight. Do you like a one party system or a multi-party system?"

These were the last words spoken by Myanmar military leader General Nay Win in a public speech directed towards the citizens. General Nay Win ruled over Myanmar for nearly 27 years with his military government. During his rule, General Nay Win enforced a dictatorship over the citizens of Myanmar. He was one of the most vicious dictators the world had ever seen.

The meaning of this quote held much anger, rage, threat, and viciousness towards the citizens. It held vulgarity, and disrespect. General Nay Win used weapons, and the power of the military to clearly enforce his control over the lives of the citizens.

The speech was directly televised on national TV for all the citizens to see. His words shocked the nation, and citizens became deeply fearful of the military leader. The older citizens were shaken that a leader would speak in such a way, calling him vulgar, rude, and disrespectful for threatening the nation. There had never been a leader in the history of the world that spoke with such harshness towards their own citizens.

Elderly women became worried for the future of the nation, and began to prepare and save up food and other resources in case something bad occurred. Students and the younger population were worried about the schools closing because it would affect their education, and in turn, their future. Everytime turmoil in the nation occurred due to strikes and riots, the military would viciously abuse the citizens in retaliation for their insubordination, torturing and shooting down protesters. Numerous protests and strikes that had occurred before made people become familiar to how things would go once citizens began to protest. Students made up a huge percentage of the protesters, and so everytime strikes would start up again, the military's first priority was to put them down.

Buddhist monks prayed for the nation to become peaceful and played a role in easing the worries of the citizens by preaching reassurances and warnings to the people.

All workers, farmers, merchants, and laborers worried for their business, and for the safety of themselves and their families. Parents warned their children to not go outside and be careful of everything in case trouble arose.

For nearly 27 years, Nay Win had abused and enforced his dictatorship over the citizens viciously. Yet he had never openly and explicitly threatened the citizens, until now. He had finally shown his true colors. Myanmar's socialist party had guidebooks which spoke of many rules, policies, laws, philosophies, and ideologies that looked perfect on paper but in reality when practiced was completely the opposite of what they had promised. Myanmar was a religious nation; everyone practiced Buddhism. The socialist guidebooks referenced Buddhist philosophies and were drawn from mainly Buddhist ideals which served to satisfy the citizens, and allowed them to be tricked into believing that the government was good.

Though the nation was ruled by a military government, militaries are meant to be disciplined and diplomatic. Nay Win's military was not any of this, and the soldiers were vicious and barbaric, using bullets to shoot down any citizen who opposed them. They were violent and self-serving, not caring for the citizens and used guns and brutality to solve any problems. Myanmar's military was not for the service and protection of the citizens anymore; it had become Nay Win's personal army for his beck and call.

His question of whether the citizens wanted a one party system or a multi-party system was not a blind threat. It had meaning for the future of the nation. During meetings, central members of the government were to vote secretly for the leader of the country. Nay Win had slipped from number 1 to 12. There was no way for him to continue being Myanmar's leader through the votes anymore, his own members had turned away from him. It was then that Nay Win plotted to keep his reign over Myanmar.

He had ruled over Myanmar for nearly 27 years, using the military for his own personal use to control his party and the nation. The fact that his own members had turned away from him was shocking. Nay Win's own actions against the citizens had led the members to see him as an unfit leader, and they did not want him ruling anymore. That's why Nay Win began to make plans to disband the party because he did not want anyone else to take over his place as the ruler of the nation.

"A gun does not shoot to the skies, it shoots straight." His words were not only an angry threat towards the citizens, it served as the beginning of his plans to take over the nation by force through the use of the military. This plan involved for him to create anarchy to make the citizens destroy each other, and then for the military to come in and stop the violence, allowing Nay Win to reign over the citizens again.

Do you like a one party system or a multi-party system? Nay Win already knew the citizens were against the one party system, they liked the multi-party system. He had already ruled for nearly 27 years, and now that he had fallen from the number one spot in his own party, he opened the doors for a multi-party system. In doing so, he allowed for the citizens to riot in favor of the multi-party system, effectively destroying his OWN party. It also allowed for the riots within the nation to occur for him to use in his plans. The riots were all instigated by his own people. With anarchy spreading in the nation, Nay Win planned to use the military to take over the nation once again.

That's why 8-8-88, 8/8/1988, for the ordinary citizens, meant protesting for the implementation of a democracy and a multi-party system in the country. The protesters never used violence, it was Nay Win's people who created violence during the protests, killing people and burning down government buildings. The buildings they destroyed did not belong personally to members of the government, they were public property and belonged to the citizens. That's how people knew these arsonists were working for Nay Win.

Nay Win destroyed his own party because the members were not voting for him anymore. He created the violence and destruction to occur during the citizens' protests which allowed the military to come in and take control. Because of this, Myanmar continued to have a military government, and the person holding the strings behind all of this was Nay Win. 8-8-88 was one of the biggest protests in the world, but it did not succeed in getting the citizens the democracy they wanted. Things went according to Nay Win's plans, and thus Myanmar, even to this day, is ruled by a military government. They're using old methods to ensure this system continues, but the citizens have not been able to succeed in overthrowing the military government.

CHAPTER 2
CREATION

Before the 8888 Uprisings, the military government had created many problems for the citizens. They were all created and planned out systematically. After the death of university student Phome Maw, there was often disputes between the students and the military government. Everytime there were uprisings, the military government would use beatings, torture, shootings and eventually kill the university students who were involved.

During this time, U Nay Win's right hand man, Colonel Aung Gyi, would purposely try to instigate riots by distributing pamphlets that depicted propaganda against the military government. To the citizens, he seemed like a hero, but in reality he was trying to create unrest.

When U Nay Win took power with the coup d'état, Aung Gyi was one of the members then as well. He was against U Nay Win, and fled overseas but then he returned. U Nay Win allowed him to be free sometimes, and other times he was placed in jail. If you look back at Aung Gyi's history, he's always been U Nay Win's right hand man, and has always followed his orders. He was placed in a special quarter in Insein Jail by U Nay Win, but that was so he could spy on what the other politicians placed in jail were planning.

(Former ministry member Tha Khin Pan Myine was also in the same quarters during this time. The reason for this arrangement was so Aung Gyi could get information from the former ministry member. Tha Khin Pan Myine had been a leading politician and organizer in the Rangoon Division. Once he became a member of the AFPFL government, he was appointed Minister of Regional Development, Democracy, and Press and Information. He was also involved in capturing the conspirator Galon U Saw, who assassinated General Aung San and members of his party. Tha Khin Pan Myine had been using the pseudonym U Min Din to investigate. He had also fought for the Burmese citizens' ownership of Thein Gyi Market. U Nay Win arranged for Aung Gyi and Tha Khin Pan Myine to be in the same quarters; he was worried about Tha Khin Pan Myine.)

For someone like Aung Gyi who's followed every one of U Nay Win's orders diligently, how can it be possible that he's against U Nay Win now? It was all according to U Nay Win's plans that Aung Gyi spread propaganda against him before the 8888 Uprisings to create riots. The citizens would have thought he was a hero, but in reality he was on U Nay Win's side. He was for democracy, multi-party system and against dictatorship but it was all a ploy so he would have supporters when he created uprisings. He declared that he would set himself on fire if there was no democracy. Once the uprisings got violent, he would back out. He slowly disappeared from the public eye, the reason being that he wasn't there for democracy; he was there to create uprisings.

During the secret votings, U Nay Win wasn't ranked number one anymore to be leader and thus he wanted to destroy the BSP(Burmese Socialist Party) to take control again. In order for him to do this, he needed there to be unrest in the nation, and thus he enlisted Aung Gyi to start these violent uprisings, making it possible for him to seize control of the nation using the military when the nation was in chaos. If he was still ranked number one, he wouldn't have wanted to destroy the BSP.

The university students who were sensitive and passionate were the leaders in the fight against the dictatorship. It was because of them that the 8888 Uprisings first started. Myanmar's university students were very loved and respected by the citizens because they were always there to fight for

the peoples' rights. In the past, there were also the leaders in the nation's fight for independence. That's why Myanmar's university students' morality, and compassion have always been important to the citizens in the nation's history. During the 8888 Uprisings, two of the most prominent student leaders who were involved were Min Ko Naing and Moe Thee Zun.

Just like there were students who were passionately fighting for democracy, there were others who were working for the dictatorship as well. These informants were in every part of the country, in every social class, to report every movement of the protestors to the dictatorship. They were even using Buddhist monks and foreigners to systematically gather information on the people who were against their rule; they were everywhere.

Everyone was involved in the 8888 Uprisings. It was the biggest citizen demonstration in Myanmar's history. Criminal activities became rampant; offices, government buildings, police stations, etc. were being destroyed. Beheadings became common. Everyone including teachers, doctors, lawyers, Buddhist monks, students, and even some soldiers and police officers were in involved in the protests. The dictatorship saw how much the citizens were against the rule. The whole world knew too. The citizens were especially adamant on non-violence and it was the people who were working with the dictatorship who instigated violence. The citizens were systematic in their marches, and were peaceful in their demonstration and protests.

The citizens were chanting for the one party system to be removed, for the dictatorship system to be removed, to get democracy, and to get a multi-party system. The citizens all believed the dictatorship and the one party system must be removed. They wanted there to be democracy and a multi-party system in the nation. The citizens had waited for almost 27 years to get this type of opportunity to demonstrate what they truly wanted. Under this dictatorship system, the citizens had been suffering mentally, physically, and emotionally for many many years. The common people were suffering, but the military members were thriving. The nation's economy was in ruins and failing. There were no medicines in the hospitals. Schools did not have enough supplies for the students to learn. Towns were experiencing blackouts often. The transportation system was broken and difficult. Farmers were in poverty and experiencing a debt crisis. Public service workers weren't being paid enough. That's why the citizens were beginning to lose their morals in order to survive because they didn't have enough anymore.

But U Nay Win had everything he needed and more. He and his subordinates got everything they wanted. They had more than the citizens in everything. 'Law' was only a word they used. In reality, 'law' meant whatever they ordered. Whatever they said was law. Their orders were law. The nation's lack of contact with the international community was not for the citizens' benefit; it was so the dictatorship could continue having power over the people. Though there is no guarantee that a nation would thrive upon contact with the international community, the citizens will be able to learn from others and thus will be able to become more knowledgeable. There will be advancements in education, and they will be exposed to new ideas and their knowledge will be expanded. However the dictatorship does not want this to happen. They don't want the new generation to have this because they themselves do not have higher education nor have advanced ideas. That's why they can't lead the nation and allow it to develop.

The dictatorship believes that in keeping their power and providing only their families with what they want and bullying the citizens with guns and weapons is powerful. They believe that controlling people through weapons and threats is something to be proud of. They don't like people who are smarter than them. They can't allow there to be people smarter than them. They control the nation through this type of barbaric ideal.

Starting from 1962, the dictatorship system has controlled Myanmar. What has occurred then?

* * *

I want to proudly tell the world, "My country is amazing, my country is rich," but I cannot. Under the democratic government, Myanmar had been one of the richest nations in Southeast Asia. Under the dictatorship system, it became one of the poorest nations in the world.

I want to proudly tell the world, "My country is amazing, my country is advanced," but I cannot. Before even talking about the countryside, even just in the capital city, there isn't enough electricity or water. Students have to study by candlelight.

I want to proudly tell the world, "My country is amazing, my country has a democracy," but I cannot. The nation has been ruled by a one party system for almost 27 years.

I want to proudly tell the world, "My country is amazing, my country has human rights," but I cannot. There is no free speech, no free press etc. When people ask for it, those people are arrested, tortured, and killed.

I want to proudly tell the world, "My country is amazing, my country is peaceful," but I cannot. People who see the soldiers are already afraid. People who see the government members are already afraid. The lives are citizens are filled with worry and suffering.

So now the Burmese citizens are hungry. They are hungry for prosperity, they are hungry for development, they are hungry for freedom, they are hungry for human rights, and they are hungry for peace and democracy. That's why all the citizens are ready to be against the dictatorship.

In this situation that's on the brink of explosion, the dictatorship has threatened the citizens using weapons in order to control the situation. U Nay Win has fallen in power. He doesn't want to give up his power to someone else. That's why he's creating uprisings in the nation. Because he can't have power, he doesn't want anyone else to have it either. Under his control, the nation was not able to develop. He took advantage of the country and its citizens. Because he's fallen in power, he's afraid. He doesn't want to take responsibility for the problems he has caused in the past. He'll destroy the country through the use of riots, uprisings, and criminals. And then he'll have the military step in and rebuild it again the way he wants it. They're using the army this way.

CHAPTER 3
CONCLUSION

I understand why he wouldn't want to give his position to anyone else. Since he's ruled for over 27 years, I understand why he wouldn't want to give up now. However the state's power is not for a person to own. It's something you can gain only by being chosen and elected by the people. The world agrees that elections are the way to choose leaders. The world has accepted this as the truth. That's why nations all over the world conduct elections. The dictatorship system will not last because it goes against the ideals wildly accepted.

Demand for change is not the fault of the people who demand it. The current situation calls for change and therefore there needs to be change. If the current situation benefits the citizens, no one will demand for change.

Myanmar's military rule has lasted for over 50 years. Under their control, the country has become broken. There is no democracy, no human rights, and no freedom. That's why people demand for change in Myanmar.

The military government is afraid to change because in the past, they've committed atrocities against the citizens. Their fear for retaliation from the Myanmar's citizens is unneeded and offensive to the Myanmar citizens' character because the citizens are not as barbaric as the government seems to think they are. Revenge continues to breed hate forever. It's the wrong thing. Punishment and justice serve to satisfy the victims. However it is not an equal payment for the victims because in Hammurabi's Law does not exist in Myanmar. That's why they must negotiate with the citizens to create peace that satisfies the peoples' desires.

Right and wrong are facing the opposite sides of each other. A wrong can be fixed to become right. When I asked myself, "What is truth?," the answer was that a truth is without wrong, and is accepted by the majority. If it is against the majority, it cannot be right. That's what I believe democracy is.

If you look at the world's history, slavery, feudalism, colonialism, fascism, dictatorships etc. once they went against the wishes majority, revolutions occurred to overthrow it. Because of revolutions, these systems failed. These revolutionaries are regarded by the rulers as less; they are seen as poor, and undignified. The people who are ruling have everything; money, weapons, and power. They are a minority. This small group of rulers when they dissatisfy the majority end up causing revolutions. This starts change. That's why I believe a "truth" must be accepted by the majority.

In Myanmar there's only a small group who does not want change. They have everything they need and want, so they don't want things to change. However a majority of the citizens are suffering and so they demand for change. A revolution for democracy is occurring. These politicians are military members who've only changed their uniforms. This isn't real change. They are still the same military government that has ruled for so long. Even if a snake sheds its skin, it still has the same poison.

There must be change that the majority in Myanmar accepts. There must change that the people desire. There must be new ideologies. There must be acceptance for change. We must welcome the new system. Be kind to the citizens. I believe this will develop a peaceful nation.

CHAPTER 4
EXPERIENCE FROM HISTORY

I will always remember the day the uprisings began. I was riding the No. 8 bus back from Insein Township Courtroom. My office was on Suu Lay Pagoda Road; Hin Tha Studio. I could hear the drivers waving and talk loudly to one another at one of the junctions, but I couldn't make out the words. Insein Road, Pyi Road, and U Wee Sara Road were filled with people. Usually there wasn't this many people on the roads. Before the bus made it to my office, the bus stopped at San Pya Station. The bus driver told us all to get off and walk the rest of the way because there was a protest going on in the city and he wouldn't drive there. I had never seen a protest in my life, and I wanted to go see everything.

I took a taxi since my office was at the heart of the city, and I wanted to get there quickly. The other passengers consisted of students, office workers, etc. and had started getting frustrated for having their trips cut short. They were all questioning and making noise about whether or not their schools and offices would be open tomorrow. They were all walking back home, but they continued to spout distasteful words against the government. The retorts showed how the people felt about the government, and I knew they welcomed the uprisings against the dictatorship.

I asked the driver if business was going well, starting small talk. He replied that he has to pay for gas, and the owner of the car. At home he had three children waiting, and so it was incredibly hard for him. The driver said I must be making a lot of money, seeing that I was a lawyer. I just smiled and told him I was a newbie so I wasn't making as much money as he would think. He told me since the roads were blocked it'll be difficult, but he'll try his best to get me to my office. He wouldn't believe that I wasn't making much money as a lawyer and I told showed him how much I made that day. It was only fifty in Burmese currency. We made it to my office, talking along the way, and I asked him how much I should pay. He said whatever I wanted to pay was good, his car would be running out of gas and he wanted to get home quickly to his wife and children. I gave him twenty-five out of the fifty I had in my pocket and he thanked me. I told him that I was thankful that he would drive me during a difficult time. The amount I had paid covered for my trip and then some. I saw the driver's happy face, and he told me he'd visit my office. I told him I'd rather him not because the only time people came to lawyers was when they were in trouble, and I didn't want him to run into into any problems. I said good-bye and got off.

My chamber master, Maung Than Dine(writer and lawyer) and U Than Nyunt were waiting outside my office. I waved to them. Just at that moment, I could hear the loud cries of protests and demands coming from the demonstrators who were marching along. The streets were filled with bystanders who came to look at this sight.

I asked my chamber master where this demonstration had started. He told me that this wasn't simply a demonstration.

This was the beginning of a revolution.

I asked him what we should do about it and U Than Nyunt laughed and told me to just follow what they'd do. Rangoon's Bar Association had planned for demonstrations to occur and in the evening a notice had been released by lawyer Daw Myint Myint Khin, in defiance of the dictatorship. My chamber master told me about his political history, and he told me tomorrow the lawyers association would be meeting and I'd better come. The citizens who were looking on the demonstration offered the protestors food, money, and water in support.

The next day, I went to Rangoon's Bar Association as I was told. The lawyers were planning what they'd do for the demonstration. A committee was being formed and it took half a day for them to decide who'd be the leader. Everyone wanted to be the leader so the decision took forever. In my opinion, I felt that we didn't need a leader yet. Everyone wanted to protest, so that was the important part. The most important thing was that we were all against the dictatorship system. There was no need to follow a leader right now. That was just what I had been thinking then. I knew if I told the others, I would be in trouble though because some people felt like the position of "leader" was something they had to have. Before even talking about a national leader, it was already troublesome picking a leader for the protests.

Maung Than Dine, my chamber master, and over twenty other lawyers began protesting. I was among the numbers. While protesting, I thought, "Is this a revolution?" and it was something that I personally experienced that day. I was satisfied with that because I was fighting for what the people desired. Day after day, more and more protests were occurring in the city. People of all classes and occupations were involved. In some instances, even police officers and soldiers joined.

During that time, President U Sein Lwin stepped off of office and was replaced by U Maung Maung. After U Maung Maung stepped in, he ordered the shootings against the citizens to stop. I was living in Yankin during that time. Somedays I could see them bring the bodies of students who were caught in the crossfires as they were protesting. I was shaken to the core by the bloodied corpses of the young bodies, and other people who saw them were furious. It made their relations with the government worsen and their hatred for the military government grew.

I was living temporarily in Kyike Pe Monastery in Yankin Township. My uncle was a lecturer for the young Buddhist monks there, and since the numbers were growing, I had to help take care of the upkeep. From seven to nine, I was the clerk at the Local Authority Office(General Administration Department of Homeland Ministry). In the daytime, I was a lawyer. During the demonstrations, I went to the city every day to participate in the protests. All the offices were closed by then. I would retell the events that were happening day by day when I came back to my town. The local security was of course by the local people.

In my neighborhood, there were two corporations that were owned by the locals; The Township Authority Office, the warehouse, and my office as well. These buildings were all in my territory. During this time, the security was controlled by the Buddhist monks. That's why for me it was easy work. I could work together with the monks and there were no problems.

We received news that some outlaws had broken into the offices and the warehouse. Together with the monks, we discussed for ways to protect the peoples' properties. I had already prepared beforehand. I had given my offices' key to one of the local judges. I told him that if there was anything important, someone could only take out the key if they had my signature. That's why I sent for the monks to get the keys. Together with the monks, we took over the buildings and replaced the government flags with religious ones. The public properties were saved. Some monks were angry and wanted to burn the buildings down but I told them not to because it wasn't government property, these belonged to the citizens. They wanted to at least burn the portraits of the government leaders, and I allowed that. Because of the monks guarding the buildings, they were not destroyed and were left in perfect condition.

CHAPTER 5
DISAGREEMENTS

After the ceasefire, there were many public political speeches and discussions taking place all over. They were mostly held in colleges and schools. The speeches talked about being against the dictatorship, and supporting human rights and democracy. I went along with my chamber master and thus was able to experience many of these events. I was able to meet and listen to the words of many writers, political leaders, lawyers etc. This allowed me to experience new ideas and learn from them.

During the time, some politicians formed the General Strike Committee. They wanted five representatives from the Lawyers' Association. U Than Nyunt and four other lawyers went and I was taken along as a follower. The committee formed at Tha Yet Taw Monastery. The chairman was a Buddhist monk.

The vice chairman was U Than Nyunt. The general secretary was a medical student.

Across the street from the Tha Yet Taw Monastery was the Rangoon General Hospital. Aung San Suu Kyi and her followers were forming their own committee there as well. Many of the lawyers who I was friendly with who were my mentors were in the committee.

A few days later, the leader of the AFPFL, U Nu(former prime minister), declared that he was forming a separate government. We received his letter of declaration. That evening, members of the General Strike Committee including the chairman, vice chairman, and the general secretary went to see Aung San Suu Kyi at her home. I was waiting in the car.

When they came back, the relayed what Aung San Suu Kyi said. **She said because there is a government currently, it's too early for another government such as U Nu's to be formed.**

A few days later, the military government took control over the nation. The Law and Order Restoration Group was formed by the military government. They began to seek out and capture people who were involved in the protests against the dictatorship. They said they would allow there to be a multi-party system. Politicians began to form countless groups in order to be elected. Many others fled and went into hiding. Some joined the ethnic revolutionaries. No one was sure what the nation's future would be. Day by day, negotiations and meetings were being held.

During this time, the military government and the citizens were on opposing sides. The people had a greater number. I believed that this shouldn't be just about different political parties; it should be about the citizens and the nation as a whole. Firstly, a government that consisted of the citizens from different classes who were leading the protests against the dictatorship and the military as well should be formed. A temporary government needed to be formed first. However the politicians did not want that, and being just a follower back then, my opinion wasn't taken into account. My idea was that a temporary government should've been formed first, and then the multi-party political system can begin to take place.

During the time, I went along with U Than Nyunt as he went to visit the former prime minister; U Nu. He visited often and they discussed the future of the nation. U Nu wished to form his own party and enter the elections. Personally, I was not interested in political parties at the time so I only went along to observe what my seniors were doing. Some members of the army contacted U Than Nyunt and other politicians, wanting to set up a meeting. They wanted to meet at Colonel Aung's home at Bahan Township, on Win Ga Ba Street. (Colonel Aung was part of the group of thirty soldiers, including General Aung San, who were actively involved in the fight for Myanmar's independence.) Before the meeting could even start, we could hear army trucks and loud whistles blocking the street. We fled. U Than Nyunt and I walked up the street normally and the soldiers checked us, but they didn't find anything so we were allowed to go on our way normally.

My previous office was in Hin Tha Studio. There was a bakery that was open during this time in front of my office. Because this was during time of political turmoil, the soldiers were always in and out around the streets 24/7 for security purposes because this area was at the center of Rangoon, the capital. Captain Nay Win Myint was friendly with us and often hung around the office to talk and rest. He made friends with the owner of the studio. I knew it was because there was a lot of lawyers working here that the captain wanted to keep watch. U Than Nyunt and other senior lawyers often came to the studio to hold meetings about the political parties. I was not interested so I gave them the rooms to use, but I wasn't involved.

I became worried because the meetings were becoming frequent, and the military was keeping a close watch. So one day, I went in to listen during one of the meetings. They wanted to join political parties and become involved in the nation's politics. They were planning on sending many of the students who were involved in the protests to go with the ethnic revolutionaries. I objected to this because these students were not professional soldiers, they wouldn't stand a chance against the army. In the forest, the weather and conditions would be very harsh. They could contract a disease and become ill at any time. How could we guarantee for sure that things would work out with these revolutionaries? I felt that it was too dangerous, and objected to this idea.

In the future, who was going to take the positions in government; the lawyers in the office right now, or students fighting against the army in the wild? Obviously we ended up having a disagreement. I didn't like what they were discussing, I didn't like what they were planning, and I told them to not use my studio for their meetings anymore. The military was keeping a close watch anyways, so it's dangerous for everyone involved.

If anyone is planning on taking a position in government, it's only fair for them to fight against the army as well like everyone else. They shouldn't be using the youth to fight in their place when these kids weren't going to be the ones that would be allowed to take office.

If someone wants to change the army, instead of fighting each other, it's better to join the army and cause change there yourself.

What I wanted was not a military government. Firstly, people who were involved in the uprisings, along with the army, and representatives from all social classes should all be put together to form a temporary government that was fair and gave voice to all parts of the nation. I didn't trust the military government, and the political parties that were being formed to participate in the elections would sooner or later end up under the military's control. It was with the military's permission that these elections were being allowed; they have control. No one can be sure of what they had planned for the future.

However no one backed me up on my ideas. I didn't have much experience, and I was young then. I felt alone. I continued to work for the public service and the General Administration at night, and worked as a private lawyer in the daytime. I didn't like the political party system at this time. I was also against fighting against the military in the jungles with the revolutionaries because in the end, it would be brothers fighting against brothers. That's why I ended up choosing to continue on my old path.

CHAPTER 6
GENERAL ELECTIONS

In 1990, General Saw Maung declared that he would allow the elections to occur, and the winner of the elected party would have power transferred to them. The soldiers would return to their barracks. He promised this, and we began to prepare for the general elections.

I was the secretary of the election committee at my local town. I took responsibly of listing the ballots for voters along with the local teachers. This was the first time I had participated in the general elections, so I was very active and looking forward to it. In the last 27 years, there had only been one party, and a ballot with two checkboxes in black and white. Aside from the BSP (Burma Socialist Party), there had been no other candidates. Even if we didn't like the person we were voting for, the next person would be from the same party as well. It was like only one person was allowed in a race, and so they always won first place.

After 27 years, there was finally a general election occurring. All the citizens were looking forward to it, it was the first in so long. The election days had arrived.

In my life, this was the first time I had experienced an election, this was the first time I had a duty to do in something like this, this was the first time I was voting, and so I was extremely happy and excited. In order to ensure the elections would be fair, trustworthy members of the community were there with the polling booths. Law enforcement, soldiers, and government members were forbidden from going into the voting buildings; they were outside as security. My voting building was at the Number 2 High School in Yankin Township. Before the doors even open, there was a huge line of people waiting outside. The noise of conversation was prominent. Just by looking at the citizens' faces, you could tell that they were excited, active, and very happy. They felt free. I felt the same too.

Even now, I can recall the feelings I had felt back then in that moment. 'This is what a multi-party system felt like?' It was like waking up from a dream after a long time. I was overwhelmed at seeing all the hope and excitement on the people's faces, and even I had shed some tears that day. These tears were for all the people that had fought and lost in their fight for democracy, the ones who were locked up for fighting, the ones who were in the jungles, the ones who were in the refugee tents, the ones who were in foreign nations; I was sad they weren't here for this moment. We have to thank them. If they saw what was happening, they would be immensely happy.

The people who had lost their lives in the 8888 Uprisings, the people who had been arrested, tortured, and taken away, I wished for them to see this now. In that moment, my heart was filled and overwhelmed with all the emotions. In my head, I could recall the protests and demonstrations I had experienced. Just then the doors finally opened, and I announced to the citizens who were waiting in line for so long, that it was time for them to vote.

The roar of cheers and the simultaneous, "HEEEY!!," that came from the citizens was immense and powerful. It was extremely loud and I understood that it was the sound of people who had been waiting to release it for so long. The sounds touched my heart and moved me to tears. The tears would not stop so easily. It was one of the happiest occasions. These feelings, these tears, this heartbeat, came from my experiences.

I'm sure there were people who were more overwhelmed than me. Some people had lost their families, some had gone through torture and persecutions. Some were suffering from the dangers of the jungle, some held weapons and were still fighting, and some had family members in the refugee tents. Some had their families split and divided across nations. I truly believe that these people felt so much more than I did at this occasion. How could we ever repay for their losses? There can never be a substitute to replace what they have lost. These revolutionaries fought not only for themselves, nor their family, nor their friends and peers. They fought and sacrificed for all of Myanmar's citizens. I wished that they could be here at this moment. I wish for them to see and personally have this opportunity to vote. But they could not reach it to this moment. The citizens who are given this privilege now owe their thanks to them. Some protestors cannot be here right now. They don't have this opportunity to vote anymore. Some have sacrificed their lives. Some have been split away from their families. Some aren't in this nation anymore. This is incredibly heartbreaking.

When the voting was done and over, the ballot boxes were brought to town hall to count the votes. The citizens waited impatiently, worried for the results since they didn't trust the military government. They feared the military government would manipulate the votes. During the 27 years in which they ruled, the military government had done as they wished, often times against what the citizens desired. For this reason, the citizens were worried.

However, a fair election did occur. The military

government did not influence the elections in any way. The NLD Party had been elected by the people as the winner. On that day, all the citizens of Myanmar joyously celebrated. After so many years of waiting, they truly believed that this day of change had finally arrived. But true change did not come. The military government began negotiations with the NLD Party. They were trying to control the elected party. They started to change the laws to delay the transfer of power to the winning party. The military government began to implement laws the NLD Party could not accept. In the end, the NLD Party disagreed and left.

After that, the military party placed the leader of the NLD Party, Aung San Suu Kyi, under house arrest and jailed other politicians as well. The reality was that the amendments done to the constitution was not for the military government to establish, it was the responsibility of the elected party. And yet the military government forcefully seized control and changed the constitution the way they wanted it to be.

The arrest of Aung San Suu Kyi and other prominent politicians caused outrage within the population. The citizens were angry, and shocked. The elected party that the citizens had all chosen had been jailed, this wasn't supposed to happen, it wasn't right. The military government went against the desires of the citizens in the worst ways possible. All the citizens' hopes and dreams were shattered. The elections meant nothing now.

The happiness of the citizens lasted just a moment. After the joy, the nation was plunged in darkness again. Everything the citizens had hoped and prayed for would not be realized, everything was back to the way it had been before. The smallest bit of faith and trust the citizens had left in the military government was gone. The citizens' disgust for their government grew even more than before. The military was not for the citizens anymore, it belonged to the dictatorship,; a small minority in the nation. A gulf between the citizens and the army was created, almost as if they became enemies. Even to this day, the military rules the nation of Myanmar.

Fortunately, I had the opportunity to come to America. For my own future, I was struggling and working hard. However my thoughts still went to my mother country, and especially to the small village in which I was born and raised in. I missed my friends, my family, and the Shwe Da Gon Pagoda. I always listened for news about Myanmar, good news about the transformation of my country. However I myself could not do anything for this transformation. I always thought about what I could possibly do to help my country. I knew I alone could not ask for change because the military government went against even the desires of almost 60 million people, refusing to listen to their wishes.

But Myanmar is still a part of the world. I wondered what groups, organizations, and what leaders could help Myanmar when it was in so much distress under a tyrannical rule. I realized the United Nations and some world leaders could help. I believed they would be able to aid Myanmar in gaining the democracy the citizens desired. Open Letter to the United Nation was written and sent to the United Nations on November 1st, 2010. The letter is here below for the readers.

Open Letter to United Nation
Stop the Election and Peace for Burma
By

Ant Bwe` Heinn

Burma's Brief History

Once upon a time, Burma was a kingdom country, a golden country, and a freedom country. Burma had been a British colony. After losing a three-time war, between Burma and the British. The country's national treasure, natural resources, kingdom, peace and freedom was being lost under the colony government. Burma's people was against the colony, because the colonies were unacceptable in Burma. The British colony had control over the country for almost 100 years.

General Aung San (1915-1947)

Burma's hero was born on February 13, 1915. His name is Aung San (present, leader of the NLD Party's Aung San Su Kyi's father). He including 30 comrades went against to the British, alliance with the Japanese. He believed the colonies must be gone in the world. The reason was because the whole world couldn't accept the colonies. General Aung San drove the British colony out, 1942.But the Japanese stayed in Burma with the fascist system, when the British left from Burma. Also the country need again to drive out the Japanese. Fascists were to be gone in Burma. The whole world won over to the fascist with the 2nd World War.

General Aung San has been assassinated in Burma, July 19, 1947. That was the country's greatest lost. Because he was only one of national hero, and twilight for the country's future. He was the most sacrificed person for Burma. People still love him. July 19th is Burma's "Martyr's Day" since then till now.

Burma's Past Democracy Government

After the independence from British on January 4th, 1948, Prime Minister U Nu   (Pa-Sa-Pha-La) government lead the country. Pa-Sa-Pha-La government had a Democracy. That was why citizens had human right, peace and democracy. It was people's unforgettable experience. Burma had been one of those rich countries in south-east Asia at the time. Pa-Sa-Pha-La government showed the country's budget situation everyday in the newspapers. Burma had granted gold in world bank. But the Democracy government did not last long. General Nay Win coup d'état from the Pa-Sa-Pha-La government, March 2nd, 1962.Military government control the country presently.

General Nay Win (1962-1988)

General Nay Win was a one party absolutism in

Burma. Between Military government and citizens, there were countless problems. At the time there were food and starvation problems. And then, there was a massacre between the Indians and the Burma citizens, and then the Chinese and Burma citizens. They had started to stir up a problem. The university students had also started to protest for the Democracy, and against the military government. Many were killed. It is remembered as the 7 July Strike. Not only the military killed the university students, they destroyed the students' conference building. At the former secretary of United Nation, U Thant's funeral, many students were killed, again. General Nay Win also created problems between Buddhist monks, and other religions. The military even collected tax from the farmers, bullying them. When General Nay Win took power, he turned Burma from one of the rich countries, to poor countries list in the world. The country's whole situation did not develop better, it got worst.

Burma's army have already been changed. Not protecting for the people, for the country, and not for the Democracy. They protect only for Nay Win. That was why Nay Win controlled the country for a longer term. On 1988, at Nay Win's (Ma-Sa-La Party)Central Committee Conference, Nay Win wasn't the number one at the vote for leadership. That was why he declared to the country, "One party system, or multi-party system?" Because he could not hold on the power anyway. He already knew what people were going to pick, that was why he created the General

Strike in Burma. He started to stir up problems to the students, obviously. That strike was the biggest demonstration in the world.

His right hand man, U Sein Liwn, became president for country after he left. He did not last long, just a week. After him, Nay Win's left hand man, U Maung Maung became president for country, again. He also did not last much longer, about a month, after he left that time. The country's whole situation was already broken. They needed that reason to seize power for the army. General Saw Maung coup d'état the country.

General Saw Maung (1988-1992)

After General Saw Maung seized power, he formed the State Law and Order Restoration Council of the Union of Myanmar. He will be general election for multi-party, and then he will hand over the country to the elected party, he declared to the world. He did make the general election, May 27th,1990. The NLD party had won. But he did not fulfill his promise. He had stalled the hand-over. He is against the Democracy, peace, and human rights. It was why he stalled. April 23rd, 1992, General Than Shwe took over power from him.

General Than Shwe (1992-present)

After he took over power, he formed the State Peace and Development Council (Will be write to

SPDC in future entries for State Peace and Development Council.).He was elected party's leader. Aung San Su Kyi and many politicians have been put into jail, still now. By doing that, he went against the law, against the people's desire, against the country, against the United Nation, and against the world. He has been controlling the country for almost 20 years now. The country's whole situation was so badly, it was almost collapsing. At his time, he killed the Democracy protesters are countless. Even Buddhist monks were killed. He created problems between the Buddhist and other religions. There were many problems between the people and the army too. Because the people did not choose him. But he control the country unlawfully. He is the one of the most dictatorship in the world obviously. I didn't see stop to him effectively from the United Nation.

Selfish Behavior

SPDC has been selling the national resorts, national land, and the national treasures. They did not show the country how much profit they made keeping it a secret. They're using the motherland's properties as their property.(For example, Coco Island for China. Rich Island for casino. Like this, country's some places, he has been selling the foreign companies too.)

His grandchildren are attending school at other country, using the country's airline and helicopter for privately. His daughter's wedding dress is covered in diamonds, from head to toe.(According to an insider, the cost was 60 million US dollars.)Many of the most powerful military officers, they have done things like this too. State SPDC, district SPDC, township SPDC, village and ward SPDC, they take advantage of citizens. They threaten the citizens, torture them and bully them too. That's why all citizens are always afraid of them.

Most of the companies must have to give them money under table. General Than Shwe is one of the most richest person in the world, but the country is one of those most poorest list in the world. The granted gold is already gone in the World Bank.

Even to some of his comrades, he has put them in jails, fired them, and retire them. Because he cannot trust anybody to make his power last longer. That's why Burma's soldiers do not trust him, and they make deals with some political parties. Some of his international secret agents have been making deals with Democracy alliances. Because he has betrayed his own comrades even. That's why they're concerned about their futures. They don't know who's next.

General Election for November 2010

He declared to the world, for general election. All democracy countries cannot trust his promise, and already been denied. Because the last elected party's leader and some people were put in jail. It was an unforgettable experience to those who witnessed it. NLD party is still elected party in Burma. Now he is trying again for election. This election is out of law and unlawfully. Because people elected government is already been jailed. He doesn't think of how he can make a deal with this party. Never happened in the world something like this. Even this election was successful, he will create problems. And then a reason to seize power again. Nobody knows what they have planned. United Nation please announce to the world, this election is not going to be approved. Because this election is not legally.

SPDC is Not Qualified for Leadership

SPDC is not qualified to leadership for the country because they cannot provide what the country needs. There is not enough medicine, and not enough equipment in the hospitals. There is not enough school supplies, for education, not enough equipment and supplies for agriculture, not enough electricity for towns and cities, there have been many blackouts. There is not enough electricity for all business too. In transportation, citizens are still using old buses, and old boats since World War II. All businesses have been inflation. Motor vehicle prices are the most expensive in the world, phones and wireless cellphones too. Because, without need to, he control the trading. All government service people does not get enough salary, and facility. That's why many are the under-table, and losing character. The army has most salary income, 70% more than regular civil service. They create divide between army and public.

They go against human rights by forcing labor, child

soldiers, and torturing prisoners. He creates civil wars near the border many times. It's for his politics to play games and expending money for them. When natural disasters happen in the country, he cannot provide safety for the people. Not only that, he denies visa for international organizations, he only accepts the aid. Obviously, when the "Nargis disaster" happened in the country for example.

How to make a development for country, how to make convenience for the citizens, and how to raise the lifestyle for citizens, SPDC isn't interested. They only care about their power, and how much longer they can control to the country. They're always watching the citizens suspecting. That means trouble for anyone. Democracy, human rights and peace is not their property. Everyone have a right actually. Why they're against, why they control, why they eliminate, this issue. Everything they did to the country is out of control, and unlawfully.

Dictatorship's Future

Human life cannot be held for more than 100 years, they must die one day. Dictatorship power cannot be held longer than 100 years, must fail one day. You must consider it this way, after you die, after you fail. Your family, children, grandchildren and your property are not going to be secure in the world. Because of you.

Now is time for negotiating, time for transforming the policy. This is your moment right now. You are going to makeover the new history. I do not realize why you don't. You must negotiate to your army, your country, multi parties, NLD and United Nation, on the table peacefully. World community and all international countries will welcome you warmly. I am strongly promise you that if you will.

Now your try for general election. Maybe this election if successful, elected party will become new government. This government will trail to your crime. Because elected government is not going to be denied to the people's commitment. Maybe you face the international justice. I would like to suggest to you the country's need temporary government first. Who will be the temporary government chosen by the people. They can make an election without inference. People will trust election absolutely. You must consider this way.

Burma Army

General Aung San create the Burma army when he defended the colonies. Burmese people are so lovely to this army, because they defend to the country, the protect the citizens and they sacrificed for freedom. After General Nay Win took over the country, Burma's army have been changed already. The army as private army. Because General Nay Win use the army misleading for him. Also SPDC using the army for their power longer.

All soldiers, when they join the army promise to defend the country and protect the people. That's why the country pay for salary. This income from citizens. Now you kill the citizens, bully the citizens and torture the citizens. The army has betrayed the citizens already. It's not going to be that way. Because only you protest to the SPDC. They are rich and rich again. Soldiers are still poor. You should know that. They're soldiers, you are too. The kind of different mean unfairly for even soldiers. That's why you must stand for the Democracy, you must stand for the citizens, and you must stand for the country.

Why I Make this Statement in the World

These statements are very ugly for SPDC. I don't want to do that really. But, what you did to the 50 million Burmese is more ugly than this. I would like to say personally. "So sorry." These statements are for the 50 million Burmese, and I stand for that. The reason is the world needs to know about SPDC.I am not attacking personally. I am not against the Burmese army. I'm only against the policy. I do this for Burma's future. That's why I'm innocent, because this is the truth. I believe truth will never fail. How about you, choose the truth or not? Make a decision by yourself.

NLD Party

NLD party has won the last election. But they didn't get hand-over the country. SPDC create countless problems, between NLD and them. NLD party stay in jail now. Including Aung San Su Kyi. NLD can't take power from them, anyhow or anyway. Almost 20 years already. It's unlawful by doing that. Now they have tried again for general election. The reason is they're going to destroy the NLD party and destroy to people's desire. They cannot do the election without NLD party's decision. Because NLD is still the elected party in Burma. You cannot remove the elected party without law. You must have to negotiate with the NLD party.

Must Have Good Relationship Between Government & Public

Any government and public must have a good relationship. If not, no country is going to develop. No business, nothing. It will collapse. That's why all countries needs peace. I believe peace can be made for everything. Now it is already a new century. World community, and everybody have open eyes and open minds already. That's why, unlawful government and dictatorship is unacceptable in the world. All international countries and world community, desire for peace always. Because can't do nothing without peace.

Who Supports to the SPDC

SPDC has been here for almost 20 years because some country supports them. I would like to say deeply, please stop. Because your support for SPDC, as bothered the 50 million Burmese citizens. Please do not support the SPDC, direct or indirect. You will be an accomplice, if you do not stop. The United Nation should know already which countries supports SPDC. The United Nation should stop these countries who are supporting SPDC. Because they are also against Democracy, human rights, peace and will be dictator makers.

ASEAN

Burma has ASEAN membership already. How to get this ASEAN membership, I do not realize. Because the SPDC is always a bother to its 50 million Burmese. They are not the official elected government. They are against the Democracy, against the human rights, against the peace, and against the world, obviously. Even to qualify for ASEAN membership. What kind of rules and regulations ASEAN have, please show to the world. Does ASEAN stand for SPDC, or the 50 million Burmese people?

Some Countries Take Advantage of Burma

Obviously military government has no Democracy, no human rights, no peace, no security and not a lawful government. That's why some countries cut business between them and SPDC. But some countries have taken advantage of Burma already. They do business with SPDC, without competition. We can see these countries are supporters of SPDC and makers of dictator. The UN needs to stop these countries effectively. Whatever they make a deal with SPDC, it is not legally. The next government cannot approve that, because SPDC is not the official government. Will avoid automatically. Please concern about it this way.

We are Together, Please Join Me

I would like to invite the world community, everybody who want peace, human rights and Democracy. Please join me, because the world is already open now. Nobody can be locked. We can communicate each other a few minutes. We can go around the world a few days. Whatever different country, government, religion, language, nationality, culture and color, one thing is same, we are human beings. We share the breathing air. We share the water. We share the food, and we live in this world, that's why we are together. All human beings need food, clothes and home, and all human beings want to be healthy, wealthy and peacefully. Human beings want to love each other. They don't want fight. These desires, you can't get without peace. Peace is loving each other, and taking care of each other. Who is going to stop these ways? This is for the world, for everyone and for Burma. God will agree with this. Because God show to human beings for love each other.

Everyone have Democracy, human rights, and peace actually. Nobody can take them away from human beings. Whoever against these ways. You are the world's enemy, the world's disaster and out of human being. We need to remove dictatorship from Burma, effectively from the United Nation. Please help my message, because we are together. This is only one world that we live in.

Burma is Not Some Other Planet

Burma is one part of the world. Not another planet. Burmese people are not from other planet, including world community, human being too. That's why Burma's issue is world's issue. Also world's desire is Burma's desire too. World is a Democracy system now. The world is against dictatorship too. All international community agree with Democracy. Not agree with dictatorship. That's why dictatorship must be removed from Burma. I request to the world community. Please help to 50 million Burmese to freedom. Because military government stay in Burma almost 50 years now. Nothing get better. Almost collapsing. That's why Burma need freedom from them.

Why Don't We

When world needed to remove colonies, the world have won. That's why most countries have Independence Day already. When the world needed to remove fascism, the world have won too. Because we help each other and taking care of each other. This is unforgettable history in the world. Now world need remove dictatorship in the world. Time for Burma. Because they have had their time for 50 years. This must be over. I believe we can remove dictator from Burma if we have international support. Only Burmese people cannot be against to SPDC. Because they have enough bullet for 50 million Burmese.

World's Future

All human beings, live in this world. It's real. All countries need elective government, not unlawful government. State power is from the people, and by the people. Not from weapon. All human being will create to the most powerful weapon in the world. If power from weapon. Is not a good thing for world's future. Time to stop dictatorship now. Because dictator virus is very dangerous to the world community. As long as dictatorship is in the world, there is not going to be peace.

Please Don't Vote

They try to lie again with this election. Please don't trust them. The election is not legally. They cannot do election without NLD party, because NLD party is still the elected party, SPDC isn't the elected government. This election is broken procedure and out of law. The country need first temporary government for a fair election. They have "kyant-phut" adopted party. They prepare for won this party. Because "kyant-phut" and SPDC is the same. You don't like SPDC, and you're against SPDC, you don't need to follow them. The country need elected party for vote over 50%.At least 20 million need to vote. They have not enough vote for election. If all citizens not going to vote. They cannot have form for their adopted government.

All citizens have right, vote or not. I would like to say not to vote. When you wake up that day, eat breakfast. Make a delicious lunch, and make a dinner for friends and family. And then go to sleep well. This is your holiday. Make a party. Will be one of those national holiday for future. We can call "New Burma Day". Stay home, don't go anywhere peacefully. They cannot kill you, they cannot arrest you, and they cannot force you to vote. Because the whole world, all international country, embassy, and all media are all watching them. I can see satellite too. Whatever they say, you must say "yes", before the election. Please do not go against them. They are already political suicide for themselves. Because they have broken the law already. I have been waiting this day for a long time. Time is come now. This is your turn, and your moment. You stay home only one day. Will change Burma forever. Their election must fail. Their adopted party must fail too.

My campaign is not bring you on the street for demonstration. Not bring you for fight. Not bring you for war. Please just stay home, not going to vote. This is very important for Burma's future. Please follow me. Don't go to vote. Make "New Burma Day". I am negotiator, I am peacemaker and I'm always stand for country.

Burma Need First Temporary Government

Military government never keeps promises obviously. They lie to the citizens and they lie to the world. They have been here almost 50 years already. Even SPDC almost 20 years. They keep power, control the country, kill the citizens, bothering the people and against the UN. Nothing more. They don't care about the world. This situation is not going to be in the world like this.That's why whatever they promise to the general election, how can we trust SPDC. Nobody know what they have planned. Because they don't want hand-over the country to others, except themselves. That reason make for temporary government first. Choose from citizens who believe in temporary government. Then the temporary government is make to the election, hand-over to the elected party, make a deal with international countries, and promise to the UN. This kind of process is defiantly needed for Burma.

Please Fix to Burma

I request to the United Nation, please fix to Burma. 50 million Burmese need Democracy, human rights, peace and freedom. I believe this can be fixed from only United Nation. SPDC is already against the United Nation obviously. This situation cannot be accept in the world, and in Burma. When United Nation fix to

Burma, no need for war. No need for fight. No need for blood. No need for arrests, and no need for revenge. Can be done on the table negotiating peacefully. World will believe to UN. And you will.

My Message

When I make these message, I have no color, no party, and no influence. I stand for 50 million Burmese. And stand for peace all human beings. I believe this message can be make a peace for everyone, peace for Burma and peace for world. We can create peace empire to this world, together.

I believe Burma must born again

Ant Bwe` Heinn

Peacemaker for Burma

Copies to

Most international leaders

Please push to the United Nation about Burma's issue.

CHAPTER 7
UNITED NATIONS

The United Nations was formed to keep peace in the world. The Security Council is responsible for international peace. But there is no peace within the government and the citizens in Myanmar. The elected party the people had chosen was put in jail and the military government rules the nation forcefully against the wishes of the citizens. Does the United Nations allow this to happen? I believe there is no excuse for this. I believe the United Nations has responsibility to aid Myanmar. I believe the United Nations has the power to help the citizens of Myanmar. If the United Nations cannot do anything about Myanmar's situation, it's the same as the United Nations not existing because it is doing nothing to help.

The people in this world depend on the United Nations to keep peace. The people have hope in the

United Nations, and endorse them for peace. Council members consist of international leaders. The citizens have the utmost belief that these leaders are incredibly intelligent and talented, that they are some of the greatest people in the world. That is also why there is only one leader chosen per nation. This position is incredibly valuable to them. People have hope that these great leaders are responsible for preventing and protecting the innocent from being tortured, displaced, killed etc.,.

In this world, democracy and human rights must exist. All human beings believe in this. But I'm not sure anymore. Dictatorships freely abuse citizens, there are so many people who are being killed, who are suffering, and who are forced to flee from their homes and become refugees. The reality is democracy and human rights don't complete exist for all people in the world today. Myanmar is a prominent example of this. The dictatorships use the military to further strengthen their control over the citizens. Armies terrorize citizens because of the dictatorship system. However the United Nations does not have the power to remove these dictators yet. Dictatorships are still successful in having power over nations today.

Myanmar's soldiers get their pay from the citizens. It is the citizens who provide the soldiers with their salary. And yet the army does not stand by the people; they instead protect the dictatorship. They have to be protecting the citizens because if there are no citizens, there is no government, nor an army. It is because of the citizens that a government and an army can exist. That's why the United Nations must take action to stop the military rule in Myanmar that is using the nation's army to further strengthen their power.

In this world, even a powerful leader such as Adolf Hitler was taken down from power. Today's dictators do not have as much power as he did back then, so it should not be so difficult to take their power away. In Myanmar, though a temporary government exists, it is still under the control of the military rule. All the citizens know that it is the military government who has true control behind the dictatorship. Today in Myanmar, democracy and human rights do not exist. Nonviolence protestors are still in jail cells, many of them students. The current government is just the military in different clothing. Everyone in power in Myanmar's government today is part of the military.

Has the world evolved today? I don't think so. Even though times have changed from the Stone Age to the digital age, it is all due to the evolution of humanity and peoples' desire to create and better the world. Inventors, creators, and scientists make the world a better place for humanity. On the other side, there are those who find ways to destroy humanity effectively. One bullet kills one person. So to kill many people, they created machines that are capable of holding many bullets. To kill even more people than that, they created chemical and nuclear weapons. If you look at history, events such as Nagasaki and Hiroshima prove just how deadly these weapons can be. Though we want there to be world peace, there is more than enough weapons that exist today that can kill all of the human population. There is currently 6 billion people living on this planet. There exists more than enough weapons today that can kill them all. How is it possible for there to be world peace when this is a reality?

I've thought about it and people do not have to be killed to die. A person will die regardless. Why are there ways to kill others when they will die one day either way? Lawfully, action must be taken. The world has changed and evolved, but it has only evolved in materialistic ways. People's empathy and philosophies has not evolved, it has lessened. Bullying, killing, and torturing are not things a sophisticated and advanced humanity would resort to. If there is no sympathy in this world between people, there can never be peace, and the dictatorship system will continue to persist and thrive.

CHAPTER 8
LAWFUL LEADERSHIP

All international leaders with UN membership must follow rules set by the law themselves too; they are not above the law. In some nations, leaders only enforce laws on citizens, they themselves are not required to follow it. That's why there is a lack of justice in some nations. I believe laws that leaders must follow should be enforced.

❖ All national leaders should be elected by the citizens. Only those who have been elected into office through a fair election should be allowed to take the position of leader.

❖ A leadership should not go against the desires of the citizens, nor against human rights.

❖ The military should not be used to further

enhance the leader's power, it should be used to protect the citizens.

❖ The military should not be permitted to arrest, bully, torture, and kill innocent citizens.

❖ If citizens are being violent, they should be punished through the judicial system lawfully.

❖ The government should always respect what the people desire because if there are no citizens, there is no government, and there is no leader.

❖ The desires and dreams of the new generation in the nation should be fulfilled and supported by the government.

❖ The leader must be ready to sacrifice their own selfish desires in order to support the citizens, and the nation.

❖ Bullying and killing own citizens, or those from any other weaker nations must not be permitted.

❖ Destroying peace by dividing the citizens through uprisings or instigating wars with other nations should not be permitted.

❖ A leader allowing the killing and displacing of their own citizens in order to keep power should not be permitted.

❖ Religion, economics, and politics should not be used as a reason to start wars within the nation, or with others etc.

Laws such as these must be enforced by the United Nations in order to keep within the world. In the case of these things happening and disturbing peace whether directly or indirectly, the United Nations must take action to remove the persons responsible.

When a leader is elected by the citizens, they must pledge and sign to promise they will uphold these values and keep peace. Only then will the lives of the people be safe and secured. A leader is a role model, and in setting the example themselves, they can inspire citizens to be peaceful.

Leaders take an oath to God when they get into office, but after that they do as they wish. In reality, God is not a witness to enforce that leaders uphold their oaths. Because they know God cannot punish them, leaders do what they want to without fear.

CHAPTER 9
REFUGEES

The United Nations do what they can in order to help refugees who are suffering. However they cannot successfully remove the dictatorships who cause these citizens to suffer. After the 8888 Uprisings, Myanmar's citizens were seen as refugees and many international countries helped them escape from the military rule. I would like to thank them for that. Just like the refugees in Myanmar, today there are many citizens who are being displaced and need help. It is with the support of numerous charities and organizations that these refugees are getting the help they need. There are more people that need help due to dictatorships than there are who were displaced due to natural disasters. I'm not saying that refugees shouldn't get help, however it is because of one dictator that so many people are suffering. And so if the cause of all this suffering is removed, there will be less people who need help.

Dictatorships do not care anymore how many people they hurt because they know the people will receive help from the United Nations and other international countries. They can do as they wish and not have to worry about whether or not the citizens who are suffering will be cared for. If this continues, dictatorships will continue to thrive, and people will continue to suffer, and the cycle of providing help to those who are suffering will never ever end. Donors providing for the citizens who are in trouble because of dictatorships will be never-ending.

In countries ruled by a dictatorship system, people are displaced, killed, and they've had to leave their homes and businesses in order to escape. The new generation loses their opportunity to go to school, many have lost their parents, and their innocence has been taken away.

❖ World leaders live securely while refugees are suffering. While leaders live in golden palaces, refugees on this earth are stuck in camps and suffering multitudes of causes. While leaders eat luxuriously, refugees are starving. While leaders wear luxurious fashion accessories and clothing, refugees are scrambling to find clothing just to cover their bodies.

❖ World leaders go to the top doctors to check

on their health while refugees suffer and don't even have the privilege of being healthy, they don't have enough medical care being provided.

❖ The children of world leaders go to the top schools and universities to be educated while refugee children can't even go to school due to their situation.

❖ While world leaders sleep on the softest beds, refugees lay on the hard earth.

❖ While world leaders conduct meetings in spacious rooms to enforce their power, refugees have no idea what the future holds for them.

❖ While world leaders happily eat and drink at beautiful parties, refugees are suffering and crying.

If world leaders were put in the types of situations the refugees are suffering in now, how would they feel? I believe if there was any sympathy, the dictatorships that are causing the millions of people to suffer would be removed.

Human beings' lives aren't secure even when compared to animals. At what level of value do we hold human lives to? Ordinary people do not have the power to wreak havoc on nations and society. They all want to have peace and keep living. The only people who are capable of these horrific atrocities are those who are in positions of power and have access to dangerous weapons. Are world leaders unable to stop these dangerous individuals? Have they given up? If this continued, the lives of human beings on this planet will not be safe anymore.

Murderers and killers will become leaders and they will have control over the world. In this world, there are more good people than bad. However that minority of people with bad intentions have much power in the world and cause so much suffering upon everyone. I believe good and noble leaders who are in valuable positions will be able to stop these tyrants. This type of authority belongs to the world leaders whom the people have elected and chosen. That's why the world leaders have a responsibility to protect the people of this world. If they are unable to do this, even if they are elected, it's the same as if they don't even exist.

I'm not against the United Nations, I'm not blaming it, nor do I want to denounce its power. I just want to see it succeed in taking care of the world and bring peace.

Thank You to the United Nations; Donors Arrested; Personal Issues

When I wrote the following chapters, it wasn't to brag, or to be prideful. I want the world to know that even honest, lawful working people are forced to face problems and go through so much hardships under the military rule in Myanmar. These are my own personal experiences.

CHAPTER 10
THANK YOU TO THE UNITED NATIONS

I would like to thank the United Nations. My grandfather (U Mwa), my grandmother (Daw Kyin Yone), my parents (U Ohn Maung and Daw Kyin Mya) and my relatives (U Htay Aung and Daw Aye Myint) donated five acres of land where a primary school could be built in my home village, Lay Ein Dan Village, Bo Ga Lay Township, Irrawaddy Division in Myanmar. I come from a farming family. My village is poor. When I was young, I'd go to the primary school nearly two miles away on foot because there was no school where I lived. Because my school was incredibly far away, I was tired when I came home. During all seasons, I went on foot. During the summer time the roads were dry so it was nice to walk. However the roads were wet, and slippery during the rainy season so it was much harder to navigate and get to school. In Myanmar schools first open on June 1st, and that was during the rainy season. Because the roads were slippery, I would often trip and fall. When I went to school, I would put my school clothing and books in a plastic bag and carry it in the rain so they wouldn't get dirty. I did this everyday. Twice a month, there would be flooding. During those times, the roads but be submerged underwater so I would have to carry my books on top of my head to prevent them from getting wet. At some places, the roads were broken and I would end up having to swim across in the water.

Because I was only a kid back then, I didn't see that that was suffering. But when the weather was bad due to heavy rain and winds, there would be flooding and I wanted to get home quickly. When I got home, I showered, ate, and as soon as I laid on my mother's warm lap, I would be asleep. This is a precious experience I can't ever describe in words. That's why I wanted to get home. I wanted to feel my mother's warmth quickly. With this in my mind, I would trip and slip my way home in the rain to get home.

When I headed out for school and I saw that it was raining, I didn't want to go. But I had to anyways. I finished primary school this way day by day. For the final examination for primary school, I had to go to a small town three miles away from my home. Students from all villages came. The small town was called Myin Ka Gone.

It was different from the village I came from. The roads were better, there were markets and small stores. Cafes and grocery stores were there as well. My friends and I were talking, wishing that our little village could be like this.

Before I knew it, I passed primary school like this. After that, I was at Myin Ka Gone from middle school till high school. After the high school finals, I went to the capital, Rangoon. I got a degree from the University of Yangon. While I was still in school, at night I worked as a clerk at the General Administration Department of Homeland Ministry. During that time, I was able to get a law diploma from a private school, and became a lawyer. Once a year, I went home to my village on New Year's. The capital and my village were very far away from each other. I would tell of my experiences as a lawyer and the villagers would all sit and listen like I was reciting a fairy tale. The younger kids wanted to be like me, and told me I inspired them.

At that time I began to hope. I thought of how amazing it would be if the new generation from my village had the opportunity to be more educated. My family began to dream of a school in our fields for the village. With that in mind, my family donated five acres for a school to be built. We didn't donate because we were rich, or we had more than enough to spare some for the village. Even though we didn't have much ourselves, we wanted to share what we had with the others. We donated the rice fields we had in order for the new generation to have a chance to be educated and learn. It was like we broke off what we were eating to share with someone else.

Though the land had been donated, there was still not enough money to build a school. The rice that came from the five acres was sold in the city to get the money, and I ran a charity in the city for the school. After that, the UNDP helped build the school because the village was poor. That's why I'd like to thank the United Nations. The UNDP gave us bricks, cement, and roofing for free, and allowed the school to become more than just a dream. The little school was destroyed during Cyclone Nargis, but the UNDP helped rebuild it again. That is why I would like to especially thank the United Nations and the international donors for their help.

Presently, the new generation in the village don't have to tirelessly walk miles and miles to get to school like I had because we have a school here now. I am incredibly happy for this. Now the children that graduated from that little school have gone on to go to universities to further their education. The school will always be here for the new generations in the future.

CHAPTER 11
DONORS ARRESTED

My fields and gardens in the village are now being taken care of by my younger siblings. The government loans money to farmers. One year, my sister did not accept the loan, but the government still came by to collect the crops. She wouldn't give it to them because she had not agreed to get the loan in the first place so there was no need for her to give anything back. She was arrested.

What had actually happened was that the local authorities had taken the loan and used the money. The villagers came to my office in the city to tell what had happened, and to recall all the problems they were facing. I was a lawyer and I could see that this was just plain bullying. I filed an inquiry and an investigation was opened. However the town's chairman threatened me and spread bad things about my character during public meetings. He would taunt and challenge me. So I went to his office to resolve the issue.

I told him that these farmers are innocent and shouldn't be bullied. The true culprit behind the loans being unpaid was the local authority, who was under his control. And why did he have to cuss and shout during public meetings? It was not befitting of a person in his position of power. I warned him if he were to continue, I would sue him. After that meeting, our negotiations went more smoothly. Under the military rule, some public service workers treat the citizens as they wish and bully them for their own selfish benefits. Even a donor like me who had provided for the village was treated unfairly. Other citizens like me have been treated unlawfully.

Wealthy business owners in the nation donate to the military and so they are favored by the government and receive benefits. They have a mutual give-and-take relationship. The media would show off the charities proudly and extravagantly. However citizens like me who have given what they could in order to support the new generations, our deeds go unnoticed under the military rule. We are not acknowledged, not even a certificate of thanks would be rewarded. It's not because we want any of this, but under the military rule the government discriminates between classes and those who support them. It's unfair, and they selfishly take what they want. If this continues, the lives of the citizens will never improve, and the nation will not evolve. Only the small minority of those who support the military will.

CHAPTER 12
PERSONAL ISSUES

I began working in the General Administration Department in 1981 at night. During the daytime, I worked as a lawyer. Ku Tha: Special Clinic, Shwe Nan (café), Thi Min Thar (lottery agent), San Di (Indian restaurant), and Boss Variety Services Law Firm were the businesses that I opened personally. When I was working, the military for whatever reason came to keep an eye on me. It was an annoyance, and frankly worrying because I might be taken away if they found me suspicious.

In reality, they wanted bribes. They don't care if a citizen is poor but if a citizen has money they will always keep watch. The military intelligence (MI6-MI12-MI14-MI26 and Navy 3) all filed inquiries on me. Even when I was not involved in any illegal activity and running honest businesses, I was still bombarded with problems. They were crossed with me because I was a lawyer and had open so many businesses and in the end I was placed in jail in the Ma Yangon

Township Police Station. Once I got to see the judge, the reason I was arrested had been for theft. I told the judge they had the wrong case, I'm not a thief, I'm a lawyer. The judge and I knew each other well, but he was under the control of the MI.

I asked for help from one of the most famous artists in Myanmar, U Sein Aung Min. He and I were acquaintances, and he knew I was honest and truthful. That's why he helped me. He talked to the military leaders about my release and I got out of jail thanks to his help. That's why in Myanmar there is no justice nor law. Only what the military government says is law means anything. They can do whatever they want. Even a lawyer like me was wrongly arrested because they were cross with me, so it's true that they can arrest any ordinary citizens they want just like me. That's why there are many prisoners who in fact do not belong there. The situation in Myanmar is very dangerous because the military government rules over the nation with the threat of violence and guns.

All the biggest uprisings and violence has always been started by the military government in Myanmar. Even students who are the same age as their own children get bullied and tortured. Ordinary citizens are treated the same way as well. Even Buddhist monks cannot escape from their violence. It is very shameful that Myanmar is being ruled under such a selfish government.

CHAPTER 13
BULLY

Bullying is the behavior of someone who holds more power than their victims. A bully can only abuse if they hold power. If this type of power was used for good, the world would be a better place. If it is being used for bad and in ways that are against the law and nature, it can become dangerous for all the people in the world. Who will it be a danger to? All the ordinary citizens living on this planet. That is why if bad people are given power, the world's future will be destroyed.

Power comes in the form of money and weapons. For someone to become powerful, they need to be wealthy and have access to weapons. Armies are built on these foundations. Ordinary citizens cannot do this, only governments can. Governments that are bad will bully its own citizens because they have access to power, they can use the army. Powerful nations will bully weaker nations because they have more military prowess. Weapons and money were not created by divine beings, they were created by humans. It is the wrong ideal to see power as a means to bully and abuse. That's why in this world once a nation becomes powerful, weaker nations become worried. When a nation has a powerful military, innocent citizens become worried.

This is occurring in Myanmar. For over 50 years, the nation was ruled by a military government. The citizens were always in fear and suffering under this tyrannical rule. Myanmar's military government uses its power to bully its own citizens, it's its only role. Has the world accepted this as the right thing to do? Is there no laws to prevent these dictators from causing suffering anymore? Are they allowing the suffering of these innocent people to continue? I'm so confused.

People can help each other in this world. Who has authority to help Myanmar? My demand is for someone or some organization to provide help for Myanmar. This is what I desire for the 50 million Burmese citizens. Myanmar's citizens are still inhabitants of this planet. They are not from another world. That's why I would like Myanmar to have peace just like so many nations are privileged to have.

CHAPTER 14
ORDER AND DUTY

The army's most important job is to follow their orders. This is a very simple mindset the soldiers have. This is a rule that is enforced throughout armies all over the world. "Orders must be followed, and duties must be served" these seem to be rules that cannot be changed. This type of ideology allows for wars, invasions, dictatorships, and tyrants to come about. If this is changed, there will be peace in the world. The world will become developed into a better place for all citizens. It's not right that all orders must be followed, nor that all duties must be served. If these orders and duties serve to hurt and destroy people, they should not have to be followed.

If we look back on to all the wars that have occurred, it was never because of the ordinary citizens. Wars were all started by the government. Empires and leaders use soldiers and armies to have influence in the world and further enhance their power. Soldiers, no matter how much courage they have, they are still human; they don't want to die.

This is the truth. In combat their enemies are people they have never met in their lives. They have never fought with these people. And yet in a war, in order to win this battle, they will kill each other. Only then is a battle deemed successful. It's the same for the other side who is fighting.

That's why after the war ends, these soldiers from opposing sides become friendly and share a brotherly bond. Soldiers are noble people. Their courage and abilities are being used by the dictators selfishly. After the wars, monarchs, kings, and dictators live wealthily in the luxurious palaces while the soldiers go back to the way they had lived before. Medals are pinned on their chests, salaries increase, but that is all soldiers get in return for their service. For this soldiers have risked and sacrificed their lives. Their courage and nobility has been wasted for the selfish needs of the people they serve. The salary they receive is not the ownership of the dictators, it is from the government's budget. The government's budget is the public's property.

Soldiers have brains but they are not allowed to choose. They have a heart, but they are not permitted to feel. Their brains and hearts have been taken out from their bodies and they act like robots, doing nothing but serve and follow orders. Whether it is right or wrong, fair or not, they still have to fight. If their orders are not fair and not right, they should not have to follow it. If they still continue to follow these orders, then they are not soldiers, they are killers.

This is happening to Myanmar's soldiers. They didn't want this to happen and yet it still did. If it were up to them, they would not want to kill innocent citizens. They are under the wrong leadership, and following the wrong orders, and serve the wrong duties. They've committed atrocities because of this. If the person who was against the dictatorship was their own family, would they look at them in the eyes and still shoot under orders? Soldiers, can you make the decision yourself? All Burmese citizens are also like family. Soldiers came from citizens.

Dictatorships are becoming more and more wealthy while Myanmar's soldiers only receive more and more hatred from the citizens. Their own citizens have lost trust and respect. The citizens have grown to regard the soldiers with disgust. It is very heartbreaking that these soldiers receive salaries from the public, and yet the citizens look towards them with hate. It is the same as biting the hand that feeds you. They have to realize that bullying the citizens is not the true duty as a soldier, and stand by the people. Instead of protecting the dictatorship, they instead must protect the nation's citizens. All human beings have principles. Soldiers are humans too. There should not be animosity between the soldiers and the citizens, they should not see each other as the enemy.

Since 1962, the soldiers have protected the

dictatorship and have only served to enhance the dictatorship system's control over the nation. Myanmar's army was only for the dictatorship system. This has persisted for 50 years, and because it's been the same for so long, they've begun to see this as "right." In this world if the wrong thing occurs repeatedly, many will begin to accept that as the right thing to happen. The soldiers must be able to differentiate between right and wrong, and only when they can choose the right thing can they truly become the people's army.

CHAPTER 15
CITIZENS AND GOVERNMENT

All countries have both citizens and government. However there are problems between the two, sometimes a little, sometimes a lot. The government consists of citizens of the nation. But once they receive positions in government, they start to become overconfident and hold themselves with high regards, causing a gulf to form between them and the citizens. Problems will start to form. They become to believe that the citizens' role is to follow what the government orders them to do.

Before being elected, leaders promise and listen to the citizens during their campaign. However once they are elected, it becomes the citizens who must listen to them. They don't listen to the citizens anymore. There is no mutual negotiations between the people and the leader. When people's desires are no longer represented, democracy does not exist. The citizens will become dissatisfied and resort to protests and uprisings. The government will then use violence to subdue them. Is it possible to allow this type of control to exist? Is it right for leaders to control the public through guns?

For example, if the people rebel against the government, the government will kill them. The citizens will not back down because they have been mistreated and become more angered. Until there is none but one left, they will resist. And until there is none but one is left, the government will kill. In that nation, there will be no citizens left. Who will the government rule then? Will they rule the birds flying in the sky? Will they rule the fish and algae in the ocean? Will they rule the frogs and mice living beneath the earth? Will they rule the lions and tigers in the deep jungles? This is impossible.

That is why the government needs the citizens in order to exist, and because the citizens reside in great numbers, they need the government to exist for there to be order. Both sides need each other and therefore a mutual respect and understanding must exist between the two. Only then can a peaceful nation be built.

Democracy exists in this world but whether or not the system has been successful in maintaining true peace is still unsure. Some nations consider themselves to be democratic, but they still do not follow the rules of democracy to the fullest extent.

The candidates have to campaign in order to be elected. They get the money from the wealthy, and when they have been elected, they must pay back. At this point, the citizens of the nation have become a second priority. That's why even though it's a "democracy," it is the wealthy who buy the government and choose what it does. The government has become a tool for the wealthy class to use.

Some governments believe that a nation will only be rich if there are wealthy citizens. The poorer class have to depend on the wealthy, and so the wealthy citizens are necessary to keep the nation running. In reality, a nation is not complete just because it has wealthy citizens. The wealthy can only invest. The economic system cannot run without the labor of the poorer classes and therefore without those citizens, the nation cannot function. That's why workers and business owners have to depend on one another.

A nation cannot be complete with just a wealthy class. The nation needs farmers, teachers, engineers, inventors, lawyers, doctors, artists, and entertainers etc., to be complete and function at its highest capacity. It needs people of all occupations and classes. Humanity survives due to specialized classes. What one can do, the other cannot. And thus they work together to mutually benefit one another. One person is not capable to completely doing everything. This is the reality of humanity.

In Myanmar, the wealthy and those with power in government work together. When money and power are combined, they become wealthy and have access to everything they want. The ordinary citizens who have neither power nor wealth have no chance to survive nor get the privileges they need. That is why those people who are powerful and wealthy cannot permit transformation and change, they are not interested in things changing because the situation benefits them right now.

Social classes are divided by wealth and money. The people at the top such as the military government do not understand what is truly valuable. Myanmar currently does not have an advanced economy. The economy is still dependent on agriculture and farming. However the government does not value the farmers and fishermen. These people are needed to mine and provide the natural resources and raw materials that go to factories to be turned into products. The capability for more products to be produced allow a nation's economy to become better.

Some nations are supportive of farming and agriculture and so these nations can have the ability to produce more goods since there is a large supply for raw materials being provided. That is why Myanmar's government must especially be supportive of its farming class, and be understanding of the nation's own citizens. They must allow transformation to occur as the citizens desire. Only when there is harmony between the citizens and government can the nation develop and evolve.

CHAPTER 16
ACADEMY AUNG SAN SUU KYI

In a film, when the villains abuse and hurt the main character, it's very heartbreaking. The actress playing the role is realistic in her depiction of pain and moves the audience to tears. She wins the Academy for her emotional performance. The meaning is the same.

In Myanmar, the military government has constantly abused the protestors and their leader Aung San Suu Kyi, who has relentlessly fought against the military dictatorship. Aung San Suu Kyi has thus become world famous for her role in aiding Myanmar gain democracy, her struggles are known and sympathized by many throughout the world. Even now she is still fighting for democracy in Myanmar. Because the world supports her in her ventures, she's awarded by many institutions all throughout the world, and even hold a Nobel Peace Prize.

However Myanmar continues to suffer under

military rule. Aung San Suu Kyi has still not won in her efforts to gain democracy for Myanmar. Because the citizens of Myanmar as well the rest of world do not accept the military rule as fair and right, they must not win. If these villains allow the transformation the citizens desire to occur, there will be a happy ending.

Daw Aung San Suu Kyi is against the dictatorship system. Yet the military government does not want to give up their power. Aung San Suu Kyi is fighting to gain democracy for the citizens, and the military government blocks her from her goal. Aung San Suu Kyi is fighting to support human rights, and the military government is against it. Aung San Suu Kyi is fighting to get Myanmar to develop and become more advanced, yet the military government is being selfish. The military government cannot win. The military government has changed their uniform to those of politicians, and the citizens do not believe them. The current government in Myanmar consists of former military personnel.

Inflation has risen in Myanmar. The daily income is in Burmese currency, however the expense are paid in U.S dollars' price. That's why all citizens struggle daily and suffer. The way things are going, the nation's economy will continue to fall and fall. The economic system will also be broken. However the wealthy minority continues to live happily in the cities, joyously partying. We cannot look at this and say the nation is okay because the majority is still very much struggling and suffering. Everytime the nation needs help, the government always has to turn to the international community. That's why the government cannot successfully lead the country.

That is why the ordinary citizens have become interested in politics, and have begun to depend on Aung San Suu Kyi as their savior. Her supporters have grown in numbers day by day. There are many tastes. Just as sweetness and sourness are tastes, so are bitterness and spiciness. Daw Aung San Suu Kyi has tasted bitterness because she had been trapped in her own home under house arrest unfairly for so many years. However the effect of that led her to become one of the most famous leaders of democracy in the world. The people that were responsible for her to become like this is the military government. But now they can't do anything to stop her. They had no idea that their actions would make Aung San Suu Kyi stronger, and that was their mistake.

In 1990, the NLD Party won Myanmar's elections. If transfer of power had been successful then, Aung San Suu Kyi would've taken office and aided Myanmar in becoming a better nation. If she was successful, after her term was completed, she would've been retired by now. If she hadn't been successful, she would've left office. Her term will end either way. Instead of that happening, the military government has only delayed the inevitable. That is why it has taken so long, until now. Regardless, Aung San Suu Kyi has still become well known more and more as the days pass.

CHAPTER 17
2015 GENERAL ELECTIONS

The 2015 elections in Myanmar will be here in November. However the military government has made it so that Aung San Suu Kyi cannot be president, even if she is elected. They've used the constitution to keep Aung San Suu Kyi out of office. The constitution was created in 2008 by the military government. That's why it's illegal. They had placed the winning party, the true elected government, in jail, and unlawfully seized power. A government that took power unlawfully cannot make an official constitution. The military government itself is not the official elected government. It's simply wrong.

In my personal opinion, I want Aung San Suu Kyi to be the president of Myanmar because when she was released from house arrest in 2010, the international community supported her in her fight to gain democracy. They gave millions and millions of money to support the nation in order for it to become a democracy. This benefited Myanmar. If Aung San Suu Kyi was able to gain the support of the international community just as she was released from jail, if she was in office she would be able to have a huge impact for the nation.

The government which does not allow for a leader that can make the nation better take office, and has done nothing to make Myanmar evolve and develop, is still attempting to keep their power. That's why this constitution must be changed. Below is the letter I sent on August 20, 2015 to the International Court of Justice regarding this issue:

Mr. Ronny Abraham
President
International Court of Justice
Netherlands

Date: 8/20/2015

Subject: Request for Removal of Amendment Preventing Aung San Suu Kyi From Becoming President of the Union of Myanmar and Request for a Fair Election Without Military Influence

Reference: In the upcoming elections, Aung San Suu Kyi cannot take the top political office due to the constitution put in place.

Aung San Suu Kyi has protected and fought for the human rights and democracy of Myanmar's citizens and has become a beloved leader in the nation. She has also made her name and cause known throughout the world, gaining the support of the rest of the world and as well as the United Nations. Aung San Suu Kyi has been supported by the world in her cause and has become one of the most famous civil rights leaders in the world.

In the upcoming elections, Myanmar's citizens will absolutely choose Aung San Suu Kyi as their leader again. Knowing this, the military government has decided to use the constitution in order to ensure that Aung San Suu Kyi will not have the chance to take top political office. This is unfair to the citizens and therefore, the amendment must be removed.

To ensure their control over the nation, the military government has created unfair laws, regardless of how much the citizens and the rest of the world favor Aung San Suu Kyi, in order to continue ruling Myanmar under a dictatorship system.

The parliament in Myanmar who made the vote against the NLD are members of the military government, whether they are army officers, veterans, or politicians under the military government's control. This central control system within the parliament allowed for the votes that were against Aung San Suu Kyi and her party.

Though the government has promised democracy to the citizens of Myanmar, in reality their "democracy" is already against the wishes of a majority of Myanmar's citizens, and therefore cannot be considered a true democracy. The constitution in place currently is already against democracy and should therefore not be considered legal.

The military government members are allowed to wed citizens and yet they also will bully, torture, and kill other citizens as well. Aung San Suu Kyi married a foreigner, but she has never hurt the citizens of Myanmar like the military government has. That's why people must stand for Aung San Suu Kyi.

Reasons

Due to the fact that Aung San Suu Kyi was married to a foreigner, and thus her children are citizens of a foreign nation, the military office has refused to allow her to take top political office. The military government made a law in the constitution that uses this reason to prevent Aung San Suu Kyi from becoming president.

Why Aung San Suu Kyi Should Be Myanmar's Leader

Myanmar's citizens have already chosen her as the true leader of Myanmar. During a previous election,

Aung San Suu Kyi and her party had already won the elections. But the military government refused to transfer power to them, and still controls the nation today.

Aung San Suu Kyi was born to Burmese parents(Father; General Aung San and mother; Daw Khin Kyi) in Myanmar, and is therefore a citizen of Myanmar.

During the 8888 Uprisings, the citizens were in need of a leader in their protests against the military government. Aung San Suu Kyi fulfilled that role and began her career in Myanmar's politics in order to fulfill the needs of the citizens.

Aung San Suu Kyi and the NLD party have never caused harm to the nation and its citizens. They've only sought to defend democracy and human rights, and fought against the dictatorship system which has caused harm to the nation.

There is no financial, or materialistic personal benefits that Aung San Suu Kyi can gain with her career in Myanmar's politics. She is only there to follow the wills of the citizens, and to fight for their rights.

Not only does she not gain any benefits from her role in Myanmar's politics, she's suffered from numerous sacrifices her actions against the military government have caused her, including being placed under house arrest for so many years.

She's suffered from physical and mental strains during her political career due to the actions of the military government who does not favor her.

Aung San Suu Kyi has never betrayed the country or let the citizens down.

That's why Aung San Suu Kyi is the true leader of Myanmar who has been chosen by the citizens. Therefore if she is elected, she should be able to have top political office and be the real leader for Myanmar.

Personal Issue

Aung San Suu Kyi is only human and that's why she has the right to marry whoever she wants. The fact that she was married overseas and thus her children are citizens of a foreign nation are all personal issues that do not, and should not, affect her political career. Marriage is a fundamental human right. The constitution cannot disallow and restrict basic human rights.

Three Generations Have Sacrificed for Myanmar

Aung San Suu Kyi's great-grandfather; U Min Yaung(alias; Bo La Yaung), fought against the British colonists and was therefore executed. He sacrificed his life for Myanmar.

Her father, General Aung San fought for the independence of Myanmar from the British colonists, and was assassinated. He also founded Myanmar's modern army, and is considered the founding father of Myanmar. He is a national hero. Martyr's Day(July 19th) is dedicated to General Aung San and his group, and is celebrated to pay respects every year.

Now Aung San Suu Kyi has fought against the dictatorship system since '88 and has spent over a decade of her life under house arrest. She has sacrificed so many years for Myanmar and continues to fight for the rights of Myanmar's citizens.

Ironically, it is the army that her father formed which has fought against her cause. It is a great tragedy that 3 generations of a family sacrificed for the Myanmar citizens so much. Myanmar's army owes a debt to this family, as do the citizens of Myanmar for all the sacrifices they have given for this nation. Therefore Aung Suu Kyi is the true leader for Myanmar.

Myanmar's Army

Myanmar's army was established by Aung San Suu Kyi's father; General Aung San, to fight for the freedom of Myanmar's citizens. The first generation of soldiers who were in General Aung San's army truly loved the nation, and fought to gain independence for Myanmar.

However since 1962 till now Myanmar's army has become the enemy of the citizens. The reason for it is the dictatorship. The whole world is against dictatorships, a dictatorship is not accepted by anyone. Dictatorships use armies to enforce rule through bullying and is a brutal, and criminal system. As long as this system is in place, the citizens and the government will never be in agreement and never be able to reach a peaceful compromise. The nation will have a broken government system and the citizens will suffer.

Ordinary soldiers do not want to fight against the citizens. They only want to do their job. But due to the dictatorship system, they are given duties that will hurt the citizens.

All nations have soldiers. Soldiers are incredibly loyal and noble people because they are ready to sacrifice for the country and its citizens. But soldiers are used to following orders, whether it is right or wrong. That's why dictators use their loyalty to further expand their power. Under the wrong leadership, they act out the wrong duties, and create problematic situations in Myanmar because of the dictatorship system.

The army is meant to protect the citizens. If the

army is murdering the citizens, then it is not an army anymore. They wear the uniforms and bear the weapons but they are not the real army. They are merely disguising themselves, they are fake. They are the enemy to the citizens if things do not change.

Myanmar's treasury and all resources are public property. The military's benefits and salary comes from the citizens. How can they act against the citizens when the citizens are responsible for their livelihood?

Universally Wrong

Myanmar's military government have made it so that the only possible rulers of the nation are military. A majority of the seats in parliament have also been filled by their own people. This system has been legalized through the new constitution and made it possible for the military army to rule with a dictatorship. A dictatorship is a broken system that no one will accept. But Myanmar's army has adopted this system and still uses it today. The world will not accept a dictatorship system because it is universally wrong.

Universal Truth

All nations have citizens. Some citizens serve in the army because the army defends the nation. An army is needed to protect the nation. Other citizens serve their country too. The government needs people to work in all the different departments to make the administration run. These employees are also working for the nation, just like the army. For_example; to take care of the citizens' health, there are doctors and nurses. To educate the new generation, there needs to be teachers. For the nation to thrive, there needs to be inventors and investors. Philosophers, technicians, engineers etc, are needed in the development to make a nation thrive. To trade, there needs to be merchants. There needs to be farmers to grow crops and provide food. That's why in the nation, the army is not the only important one. Everyone has a duty and they are all equally important and necessary to make the nation thrive. Therefore anyone has a right to leadership. They all have a right, they all have a chance, because they are all equal.

For example; if the farmers are unable to provide for the nation, people will starve and the system will collapse. They are necessary. Likewise, people have to share whatever they create with others to ensure that people are all provided with these necessities. Myanmar's military government must understand this better because this is a universal truth.

What The Military Government Has Done

The person that makes the law must act lawful themselves too. They must be clean, and be lawful.

This is a main priority. If a person makes a law for everyone to follow, but you yourself are against the law, it is unfair.

Since 1962 till now, the military government has unlawfully killed and tortured citizens that have fought for human rights and democracy, and had protested against the dictatorship. There is no law in place stating the military government is allowed to punish and kill citizens who protest non-violently against their rule.

They have sold natural resources such as rubies, jadeites, timber, etc., and rented public property, land, islands etc., to foreign companies and have not disclosed what the lands are being used for, or how much money they made from it, or how they've spent the money. The citizens never know the true numbers. They keep the money and the information to themselves and do not tell the citizens where the money is and what the lands are being used for even though it is all public property and does not belong to them. The public needs to know everything because it is their property.

Members of the military government are wealthier than they say on the papers. Their supposed income is less than the actual amount they are seen to be spending on luxuries. The luxuries they currently own such as cars, homes, land, foreign accounts etc., can be revealed in the accounts they use to store their actual money. They work together with the wealthiest in the nation to keep making money for themselves, and help each other.

During natural disasters, the UN as well as numerous agencies and other nations have donated money for Myanmar to rebuild itself after the devastation. Some military government member have taken money for themselves from these nations by making deal with the contractors.

The military government is always playing with people's desire for change. During times when change must occur, they will purposely create problems to stall and prevent the change from coming, in order to keep a firm grip on their power.

You can easily determine whether all I've written is true or not by inquiring. The military government has many many cases of corruption. But I'm not asking to take action this time, I only want for them to change their ways, and change the dictatorship system.

What I Believe

I believe there are still fair laws and justice in the world. I believe organizations such as the United Nations and the International Court of Justice etc., are there to uphold these laws and protect all. The dictatorship in Myanmar which created the constitution is only there to benefit themselves. If a majority is in disagreement with it, then it is a not a democracy. If it goes against fundamental rights, it is against human rights. That is why I believe the current constitution is unfair and unlawful, and should not be accepted.

Myanmar's military government has ruled unlawfully since 1962 till now and they have never made the country better. They've controlled Myanmar for over 50 years and yet they have not changed for the people's desires. It's very shocking that they were able to rule unlawfully for such a long time. I believe the world will able to fix that now. Therefore I make this request for the removal of the current constitution put in place in Myanmar and for a fair election in Myanmar without military influence, and support Aung San Suu Kyi in her efforts to create a better nation forever.

Sincerely,

Oscar A. Myint
P.O. Box 350420
Brooklyn, NY 11235
oscarayemyint@gmail.com

I believe you can fix Myanmar easily. I hope this copy will make you help the citizens of Myanmar and allow them the chance to create a better nation forever.

CHAPTER 18
UNITY FOR THE NATION

Myanmar has lived in harmony with its ethnic groups. Under the kingdom system, there was peace then too. Under the British colonial rule, there was peace as well. Under Japan's fascist system, there was peace. And now there is peace too within the ethnic groups of Myanmar. But because of differences in culture, there would sometimes be revolutions and such in support of separation from the mainland. One state cannot survive separately because it is small. It will need to depend on a stronger state for defense from others' attacks. However even the stronger state that is protecting it may question its loyalty because it had betrayed its mainland in the first place. That is why unity and staying together with the mainland is better for the nation.

Irrawaddy River, Chindwin River, Sittaung River, and Salween River were not created by anyone. We accept that it was there naturally. The mountains that exist in the Kachin, Shan, Karen, Kaya, Mon, Rakhine etc., States were not created by anyone. They occurred naturally. The land was not created by anyone. The deltas were not created by anyone. Even if one lives in the mountains or on the lower sides of Myanmar, they are still all Burmese. If those who live in the mountainsides came to the lower sides to work and eat, no one will turn them away. And if those in the lower sides went up to the mountains to work and eat, no one will stop them. That's why all the ethnic groups in Myanmar live amongst each other in peace.

Those that come from the lower sides enjoy and value the culture, foods, dress etc., of the mountains. The ones from the mountains regard the lower sides with the same respects as well. That's why it's better for the nation for the different states to love, respect, and care for each other mutually. It's not good for country if there are disputes between brothers and sisters. They should not be fighting against each other.

CHAPTER 19
TO THE FARMERS

There is no way to extend the life of the earth's soil with technology. There is no way to expand Myanmar's geography using technology. The earth's soil has come about from nature. I would like to request to the farmers of Myanmar who work in the fields, mountains, gardens, etc. to take care of the earth for the future generation. This soil will benefit people and provide humanity with food and resources for as long as they exist. The soil is so important to the lives of humanity.

Currently, Myanmar's government has sold and rented Myanmar's land to foreign companies, starting "projects" that in fact force out farmers from their livelihoods. Before, many farmers in Myanmar had a business using the land. Now that the land has been forcefully taken from their hands, they are now jobless. The money from selling the land is only for one instance. The land is gone forever. It will be gone to the newer generations.

The government's projects are to urbanize and develop Myanmar into a more advanced nation. However the future of the thousands of farmers in Myanmar is lost because their livelihoods that has allowed their families to survive generation after generation is now gone. The only people that these projects will benefit are the wealthy minority, company owners, and the government. The farmers and the average citizens will not gain any benefits from these projects. When the land has been taken away, these citizens will be forced to become workers. As more jobs are lost due to urbanization, more and more citizens will turn into workers which will allow the government and companies to devalue them. The citizens will not be paid fairly in the future.

If the Burmese government sold everything Myanmar had to foreign companies, it is the same as selling the nation out to them. Other countries don't even have to invade or attack Myanmar in order to have access to its resources, they can just buy it. And once they've bought it, Myanmar's economy will be completely under the control of these foreign companies, not the Burmese citizens themselves. Myanmar's citizens will become nothing more than workers mindlessly giving their lives up in the factories under the control of the foreign companies. Their lives will become one of slavery. That is why I am begging to not allow the Burmese citizens to become enslaved because the government is selfish. The government has responsibility to ensure this situation does not ruin the nation and the citizens. It is their job to take care of the citizens. In this situation, law does not seem to exist. If the government can easily come in and take away the land that belongs to the citizens however and whenever they want, where has the rights of the citizens gone? Under the government, the citizens' land and belongings are not secure. This is lawless and wrong.

The current projects only serve to create factories and taller skyscrapers. Agriculture and farming that allows the citizens to have food and resources will be lost forever. Valuable natural resources are being taken away and destroyed for the future to create room for "development." The most important thing to humanity nature has offered is food and resources. With these projects, those valuable things the land has offered will be gone. The organic and naturally grown foods will be substituted by chemically enhanced versions by the factories. These chemicals are not always healthy for people. The citizens will eat modern foods and contract new diseases. That's why the priceless natural resources Myanmar has should not ever be sold out for development.

CHAPTER 20
FREE EDUCATION AND FREE HEALTH CARE

In Myanmar, prices are going up. Everything is becoming more and more expensive. Children in poverty cannot afford to finish their education. Only wealthy children can finish their education, and become intellectuals. If we measure the future of the nation with education, the poorer children will never have access to positions in government, and will not have say in the nation's future. Only the wealthy children will be allowed to have positions in government and say in the nation's development. The children from poorer families do not have a chance, they won't have a say in their future. Only the wealthy class cannot represent nor understand the citizens from all of the diverse social and economic classes in Myanmar. This can create difficulties in the nation's future.

Doctors and medicines are expensive. The poorer classes cannot afford them, they cannot afford to look after their health and thus succumb to illnesses and injuries that can easily be treated. Lives are being needlessly lost. That's why free medical care must exist, and the government must take responsibility to look after the health of its citizens.

"Myanmar is a poor nation" is no excuse for the government not being able to provide these necessities to its citizens. The United Nations and many international communities have provided Myanmar with enough to provide medical care and education to its citizens. If this money was used wisely, systematically, and fairly, it can be distributed properly to ensure that all citizens have what they need and are not lacking in the necessities such as medical care and schooling.

CHAPTER 21
FAIR ELECTIONS FOR MYANMAR

On November 8th, 2015, Myanmar will be conducting its multi-party General Election. The military government's party is continuously taking more opportunities than the others. They use the nation's money unlimitedly for their campaigns. The elected Chairman of Commission has allowed this on the grounds that because they are the current government, they can use the nation's money however they want. He further stated to the press that if the other parties won, they can also use the nation's money like this as well. This is nonsense. The nation's budget is not the government's budget, it is the nation's. The government cannot freely spend as much as they want on whatever they want because the money does not personally belong to them at all, it belongs to the citizens. Many of these issues regarding the military government in Myanmar is simply unlawful and they can run amok with no fear for consequence. That is why I would like to present these problems to the United Nation and international leaders in order to ensure that

Myanmar's government is lawful and the elections are fair.

To: Mr. Ban Ki-Moon
Secretary General
760 United Nations Plaza
Manhattan, New York 10017

10/13/2015

Subject: Amendment of Constitution and Fair Elections for Myanmar

The military government in Myanmar has been controlling the nation for over 50 years. The preparations for general elections in Myanmar have started now. However, the constitution in Myanmar is unfair and biased towards the military government, and this is unfair to the citizens. It's just like a dictatorship.

Funds from International Community

When Aung San Suu Kyi was released in 2010, the Japanese government took away the debts that Myanmar owed to them. Australia, Germany, America, etc., provided the country with support because they were attempting to gain democracy. However, even now nothing has changed. The nation is still under military rule. The support given by the international community for democracy was accepted by the nation, but there was no change done.

Constitution

The constitution is made up of 3 groups of parliament. One group is 25% military personnel and they weren't voted into parliament through the elections, but hold a seat there regardless. The constitution ensures that military members automatically get a seat without voting. The real decision makers in the government are the military members.

Discrimination Within the Constitution

The military members have an advantage and are given more chances unfairly through the constitution. Other social classes, people who are NOT soldiers or part of the military such as farmers, teachers, lawyers, doctors, engineers, artists etc., are not given the same advantages. This is discrimination. The constitution is dividing the people. The constitution also includes numerous offenses against democracy and human rights. That's why there must be change to the constitution.

According to the history, the military says they're necessary. They're trying to brainwash the citizens into believing the military is their savior when in reality no one is being forced to join the military, and there is no mandatory military service required.

The soldiers willingly join the military and so it is their job to take care of the citizens; this is their duty. But they are using their role as the military to take many advantages from the country. All citizens are important, not just military members.

Pyi Khain Phyoe Party

Obviously the Pyi Khain Phyoe Party consists of members from the military who've simply changed their clothes into politicians'. Other parties' representatives follow the rules and present their properties and profits, however the members of the Pyi Khain Phyoe Party do not. This is unfair and unlawful because the party members own so much unlawfully.

Election Committee

The leaders of the election committee are also former military members. This is very unfair since the election committee should be neutral and not be biased, but the citizens cannot do anything about it.

The chairman of the committee stated that he will only be responsible for 30% of the votes, and does not care about the other 70%. This is the same as saying he'll make sure 30% is truthful, but he'll do whatever he wishes to with the other 70%. A person who will only be responsible for 30% of the votes should not be qualified for chairman of the Election Committee.

Creation

Currently in Myanmar, protesters, politicians, and students are being arrested and put in jail. Criminals are being freed. Because of this, there is a rise in crime so close the elections. The only weapon holders in the nation are the army and some ethnic revolution groups. Who has responsibility? The people have no weapons, and are not criminals.

The United Nations Ensure Myanmar's Elections are Secure

The elections can be delayed due to the reasons stated above. If something were to happen, the United Nations can help prevent it. That's why maybe the Peacekeepers are needed in Myanmar during the elections. The election boxes and the votes should all stay where the citizens are to be counted. Currently, the votes are taken away to Town Hall to be counted; those places are under the control of the government. During last election, they declared the actual winner as losing, and the one who lost to have won so they are manipulating the votes.

"Obama Kissed Aung San Suu Kyi Twice"

The Pyi Khain Phyoe Party candidates stated that Obama came and greeted Aung San Suu Kyi twice, kissed twice, but cannot do anything for her nation. It is a greeting, and yet they were quick to assume and make rude comments about it and jeer. How can we allow such people to have high positions in government?

The constitution itself is unlawful, unfair, divides the citizens, biased, and discriminatory. As long as the nation is being ruled using this constitution, it will gain democracy because this constitution is ruled by the military government.

That's why the Burmese citizens need help, please. We don't have another Aung San Suu Kyi. She's the only one for the country.

Truthfully for Myanmar,

Oscar A. Myint

CHAPTER 22
AUNG SAN SUU KYI FOR MYANMAR

❖ It is true Daw Aung San Suu Kyi married a foreigner, but she did not betray the country and did not treat the citizens of Myanmar with viciousness. Though the military government members married Burmese citizens, they have has arrested, tortured, and killed their own citizens in Myanmar viciously. For this reason you must vote for and support Aung San Suu Kyi.

❖ Aung San Suu Kyi is not a politician, she is a revolutionary. Politicians in Myanmar have used the nation's money to run their campaigns, and once they win they also receive their pay from the nation's budget, and after they retire, their pension is also from the nation's budget. They did not have to invest themselves in order to get the position.

However revolutionaries wish to change the old system, and thus have sacrificed for their cause. Aung San Suu Kyi has faced many sacrifices. All the citizens know how much she has sacrificed. For this reason, you must vote for and support Aung San Suu Kyi.

❖ If you look at her family history, Aung San Suu Kyi's great grandfather, and her father fought for Myanmar's independence. And now Aung San Suu Kyi is fighting to gain democracy for Myanmar's citizens. That's why you must vote for and support Aung San Suu Kyi.

❖ When Aung San Suu Kyi was released in 2010, the international community supported her with millions and millions of money to support her cause in gaining democracy for Myanmar. If she gained that much support just after being released, she would gain even more support for Myanmar if she became the nation's leader. That's why you must vote for and support Aung San Suu Kyi.

❖ After the elections, one will have to become a leader for Myanmar regardless. That leader must be able to stand with the international community to gain support for Myanmar. If that leader who has been elected by the citizens was someone the international community believed in and respected, it would be better for the nation. If it was someone else, the outcome might not be the same. If the international community is looking for a leader who is respected, well known, and favored, there is no other choice but Aung San Suu Kyi. That's why you must support Aung San Suu Kyi.

CHAPTER 23
PEACE FOR THE WORLD

All of humanity on this earth want peace. But due to dictators and tyrants in some nations, many suffer. Citizens are forced to flee and become refugees or even lose their lives. The world leaders must take responsibility to fix these problems to create peace in this world for all.

Buddha's first preaching after he became a god was called the Dharmachakra.

Ah pee yey heep than pa yaw gaw dote khaw
Pee yey heap weit pa yaw gaw dote khaw
(Pali)

This translates to:
"Staying with those you do not love is Suffering."
"Separated from those who you love is Suffering."

I truly believe that if Buddha was still living in today's world, he would see the citizens' lives under the dictatorships as Suffering as well, and preach it so.

I believe peace does not need to be searched for and studied by the top most prestigious universities in the world. Nor does it need to be searched for within the pages of thick textbooks. There is no technology that can create peace. So many expensive and time consuming meetings do not need to be conducted so often by world leaders in the search for peace.

If you don't want to die, you won't kill others. If you don't want to face suffering, you shouldn't make others suffer. If you love yourself, you will love others. If you love your family, you must love others' families too. If there is sympathy like this, it's very simple to gain peace. I hope there will be peace for all of humanity in this world.

There are still dictatorships in the world today. If these rulers were instead noble people rather than dictators, it would not be necessary for me to write this book.

Do not be angry. You must read this book. After reading, I hope you will become more sympathetic and make the world more peaceful.

www.ingramcontent.com/pod-product-compliance
Lightning Source LLC
Chambersburg PA
CBHW060501280326
41933CB00014B/2815